FACTS AT YOUR
FINGERTIPS
NORTH
AMERICA

BROWN
BEAR
BOOKS

Published by Brown Bear Books Limited

An imprint of
The Brown Reference Group plc
68 Topstone Road
Redding
Connecticut
06896
USA

www.brownreference.com

Library of Congress Cataloging-in-Publication Data available upon request.

ISBN-13 978-1-933834-07-8

Author: Derek Hall
Editorial Director: Lindsey Lowe
Project Director: Graham Bateman
Art Director/Design: Steve McCurdy
Editor: Virginia Carter

Printed in Singapore

CONTENTS

NORTH AMERICA

This volume covers the areas of continental **North America** (Canada, the United States, and Mexico), **Central America**, and the **Caribbean**.

Early Peoples

The first inhabitants of North America crossed from Eurasia about 35,000 years ago via the Bering Land Bridge. Many migrants spread throughout the wilderness areas of present-day United States and Canada, but others continued south, through Central America (the birthplace of the Mayan and Aztec empires) and on to South America (where the Incas flourished until the Spanish conquest of the 1530s). As the continent's inhabitants evolved they specialized. Some were hunter-gatherers, while others became early farmers, growing crops such as maize (corn) and potatoes. The Inuit (Arctic hunters and fishermen) did not emerge from Alaska until 1,000 years ago, when they spread eastward across Canada and into Greenland.

Colonial History

In the 1600s the British colonized the Eastern Seaboard of North America and the area around Hudson Bay. The French colonized areas of the north (in today's Canada) and of the west (the hinterland known as Louisiana Territory). The Spanish colonized the southwest of today's United States, Mexico, and Central America. All three powers colonized islands in the Caribbean. After the Louisiana Purchase of 1803, the inevitable move westward by settlers from the east, and the completion of the transcontinental railroad, Native Americans began to lose their lands and their traditional way of life.

Today's North America

The racial origins of the nonindigenous population of North America are British, Spanish, French, and African (the latter being descendants of slaves). Despite tighter immigration controls and its share of social problems, the United States is still perceived by many—as it was 100 years ago—to be the land of golden opportunity. This in turn has led to legal and illegal immigrants entering the country from Mexico, the Caribbean and Asia.

The continent's major population centers—which are also the areas of manufacturing and service industries—are on the Western and Eastern Seaboards, up the Mississippi River from New Orleans, around the Great Lakes, and in Mexico City. Vast tracts of the hinterland, however, are only sparsely populated and are given over to agricultural production or to the extraction of minerals.

Natural North America

The continental mainland is home to tropical rain forests in Central America. Farther north, in the Southwest United States, are deserts, canyons, and buttes. There are areas of forest, grasslands, and prairies as well as the tundra of northern Alaska, Canada, and Greenland. Major geographical features include the Rocky Mountains, the Mississippi River, and the Great Lakes. Despite (or because of) its spectacular terrain, the continent is never free from natural disasters. The western United States lies on the San Andreas fault, the Eastern Seaboard—including the Caribbean and the Gulf of Mexico—is subject to hurricanes, the Mississippi River is prone to flooding, and northern and central winters are harsh.

Wildlife includes polar and grizzly bears, moose, pelicans and bald eagles (the national bird of the United States). There are rattlesnakes in the Southwest and alligators in the Southeast. Offshore are sharks, turtles, dolphins, and trophy fish such as marlin. But the herds of buffalo, once "farmed" by Native Americans, have gone and now exist in limited numbers in places such as Yellowstone National Park. The only native peoples who still hunt for a living are the Inuit. Farther south, in Central America and the Caribbean, are the exotic creatures associated with rain forests and with lush vegetation.

Yosemite National Park, located in the Sierra Nevada range of California, is a spectacular mountainous area boasting huge cliffs, peaks, plunging waterfalls, and giant sequoia trees.

CANADA

The second-largest country after Russia, Canada occupies most of the northern half of the North American continent. Its culture and economy have much in common with the United States, yet Canada is distinct in its character and ethnic mix, much of which can be traced back to its British and French origins.

Geography

Canada's landscape includes: the high peaks of the Rocky Mountains range; great boreal forests; vast rolling plains and fertile prairies; numerous massive glacial lakes and rushing rivers; Arctic tundra; and many snow-clad offshore islands. The country can be divided into several geographical areas. The largest is the bowl-shaped Canadian Shield, occupying nearly half the country and centered on the Hudson Bay.

Southeast of the Shield lie the lowlands of the Great Lakes–Saint Lawrence River region, the most populated part of Canada. East of Quebec, in Appalachian Canada, craggy mountains have been

NATIONAL DATA – CANADA

Land area	9,093,507 sq km (3,511,023 sq mi)			

Climate	Altitude m (ft)	Temperatures January °C(°F)	July °C(°F)	Annual precipitation mm (in)
Resolute	64 (200)	-32 (-26)	4 (40)	138 (5.4)
Vancouver	0 (0)	3 (38)	17 (63)	1,199 (47.2)
Winnipeg	248 (813)	-18 (0)	20 (67)	514 (20.2)
Montreal	30 (98)	-12 (10)	20 (67)	1,065 (41.9)
Halifax	30 (98)	-6 (21)	19 (65)	1,542 (57.1)

Major physical features highest point: Mount Logan 5,951 m (19,524 ft); longest river: Mackenzie 4,240 km (2,635 mi); largest lake: Lake Superior (part) 83,270 sq km (32,150 sq mi)

Population (2006 est.) 33,098,932

Form of government federal multiparty parliamentary monarchy with two legislative houses

Armed forces army 33,000; navy 12,000; air force 17,100

Largest cities Toronto (4,726,194); Montreal (3,290,804); Vancouver (1,840,441); Calgary (1,013,675); Ottawa (capital - 896,048); Edmonton (841,202); Hamilton (699,795); Quebec (650,026); Winnipeg (633,107); London (350,340)

Official languages English, French

Ethnic composition British 28%; French 23%; other European 15%; Amerindian 2%; other mainly Asian, African, Arab 6%; mixed background 26%

Religious affiliations Roman Catholic 42.6%; Protestant 23.3%; other Christian 4.4%; Muslim 1.9%; other and unspecified 11.8%; none 16%

Currency 1 Canadian dollar (CAD) = 100 cents

Gross domestic product (2006 est.) $1.165 trillion

Gross domestic product per capita (2006 est.) $35,200

Life expectancy at birth male 76.86 yr; female 83.74 yr

Major resources coal, natural gas, petroleum, hydropower, iron ore, nickel, zinc, copper, gold, lead, molybdenum, potash, diamonds, uranium, rock salt, fisheries, tourism, cereals, dairy and meat products, food stuffs, timber, tobacco

eroded by weather and glaciers. Southwest of the Shield and Hudson Bay is the Great Plains area of Canada—a vast triangular expanse of level terrain covering about one-fifth of the land area. Farther west the land rises to the rolling plateaus of the Saskatchewan Plain, and west of the Great Plains is the Mountainous Canadian Cordillera that borders the Pacific coast. To the northwest barren Arctic islands such as Baffin Island and Ellesmere Island border the permanent ice of the Arctic Ocean.

Over half of the country has a subarctic climate, with cool summers and very cold winters—often colder than in the Arctic itself. Farther south the climate is typically continental, with hot summers and cold winters. The warmest summers occur in southern Ontario, and the southeast coast has the mildest winters. The northern tundra gives way to one of the world's largest coniferous forests, stretching from Alaska to Newfoundland. Elsewhere, mixed forests and broadleaved woodlands flourish. The mighty

Historic Quebec City, capital of Quebec—Canada's largest province—viewed from across the St. Lawrence River.

CANADIAN WILDLIFE

The Arctic waters support whales, seals, walruses, and polar bears. Tundra species include musk oxen, caribou, lemmings, wolves, and many migratory birds such as auks, sea ducks, gulls, and terns. Caribou flourish in the northern forests, along with moose, lynx, and brown and black bears. Beavers, martens, mink, and other species still form the basis of a fur trade. Farther south deer, squirrels, chipmunks, otters, and birds such as cardinals and orioles are found. Jackrabbits, gophers, and grouse inhabit the prairies along with bison and pronghorn antelopes. Bighorn sheep are adapted to the mountains.

prairies were once rolling grassland, but today much has been given over to wheat production.

Society

Canada's population is diverse. Ancestors of its earliest inhabitants—Native Americans—arrived 30,000 years ago, followed about 1,000 years ago by the Inuit. These peoples now make up a minority of the population. Nearly two-thirds of the people today are English- and French-speaking descendants of European settlers, although there are communities from other parts of Europe, as well as Asia. Canada's democratic government derives from that of Britain. One of its problems is the reconciliation of the aspirations of the French-speaking peoples, who form the majority in Quebec, with the different traditions of the English-speaking Canadians. Canada is also increasingly accepting its obligations toward its indigenous peoples.

Economy

Canada is rich in natural resources, with massive mineral deposits, huge areas of commercial-grade timber, and vast areas under cultivation. The resulting prosperity has created one of the highest living standards in the world. Manufacturing industry is split into two sectors: the processing of raw materials and the creation of manufactured goods. Despite having a huge and important agricultural industry, only about 8 percent of the land is used for farming.

CANADIAN PROVINCES

Canada has 10 provinces. Each of them has a governmental structure mirroring that of the nation. Provincial governments are responsible for local concerns such as civil laws, taxation, land management, trade, health, welfare, and so on. In addition, the huge but very sparsely populated Yukon, Nunavut, and Northwest Territories are administered directly by the federal government.

Yukon Territory

Covering an area of 483,450 sq km (186,660 sq mi), this is a vast, beautiful region of high mountains, dense forests, plateaus, and sweeping valleys bisected by huge rivers. Mount Logan, Canada's highest peak, is located in the extreme northwest of the territory. Summers are hot, and winters are cold. The discovery of gold in the 1890s led to the Klondike gold rush, and minerals such as gold and silver are still mined today. The forests form the basis for a large timber industry, with hydroelectric power providing much of the territory's energy needs. Tourism is growing, with visitors attracted to the spectacular unspoiled scenery. The capital of the Yukon is White Horse.

TRANSPORTATION IN CANADA

Canada's huge size and rugged, mountainous, often snowbound, landscape make travel difficult. Many northern communities need all-terrain vehicles and aircraft for access. There are two transcontinental railroad systems and provincial rail networks. There are also railroad links with the United States. In the Atlantic provinces ferries provide essential links. British Columbia has a large ferry fleet, too. The St. Lawrence Seaway connects the Atlantic Ocean with the Great Lake ports such as Chicago and Thunder Bay. About half of Canada's roads are located in the prairie provinces.

Northwest Territories

The Northwest Territories, whose capital is Yellow Knife, extend for 1,171,918 sq km (452,478 sq mi). Mountains rise to more than 2,700 m (9,000 ft) in the west and to more than 2,600 m (8,000 ft) on Ellesmere Island. Tundra extends over much of the north and east, and the possibilities for farming are therefore limited. However, trapping for the fur trade is an important economic activity, especially among the largely Inuit, Indian, and Métis (part French, part Indian) population. The main industry is mining, and it includes the exploitation of minerals such as oil, gas, gold, and diamonds. Tourism is also important.

British Columbia

This mountainous province on Canada's Pacific coast covers an area of 929,730 sq km (358.968 sq mi). The rugged coastline is punctuated with deeply indented mountainous fjords and many offshore islands, most of which are uninhabited. The most densely populated regions are around the valleys, particularly the Fraser

Canada is divided into 10 provinces and three territories.

YUKON TERRITORY

NORTHWEST TERRITORIES

NUNAVUT

BRITISH COLUMBIA

ALBERTA

SASKATCHEWAN

MANITOBA

ONTARIO

QUEBEC

NEWFOUNDLAND

NEW BRUNSWICK

PRINCE EDWARD ISLAND

NOVA SCOTIA

River region near Vancouver. The extensively irrigated southern plateau and Fraser delta are almost entirely given over to fruit growing. Vegetables and dairy products are also important, and there is a salmon-fishing industry.

The province's chief agricultural resource is timber, which is used to make wood pulp, plywood, newsprint, and sawn timber products. (Canada is the world's leading exporter of wood products, which account for 10 percent of all exports.) Most of British Columbia is covered with forests that are exploited by major multinational companies. Mining has long been important to the province, with minerals such as molybdenum forming the basis of the industry. Hydroelectricity provides most of the province's power requirements. The mild climate of the southwest attracts many tourists. The capital is Victoria, although Vancouver to the north is much larger, being Canada's third-largest city and the country's chief Pacific port.

Alberta

Alberta, whose capital is Edmonton, is the most westerly of the Canadian prairie provinces. It covers an area of 661,190 sq km (255,285 sq mi). The landscape ranges from the high mountain peaks of the Rocky Mountains in the southwest to the vast, flat prairies of the east. Dairy and beef cattle are reared here (nearly half of all Canada's beef is produced in Alberta), together with sheep and pigs. Alberta is also the leading bee-keeping province of Canada. Wheat is the primary agricultural crop, with canola and other grains also important. Forestry, particularly the exploitation of softwood, is also important. Alberta contains the bulk of Canada's known fossil fuel deposits, including oil, gas, and coal; gas and oil have attracted much recent attention in the Mackenzie Valley.

Banff National Park, Alberta, boasts the kind of scenery for which Canada is famous—rugged mountains, dense forests, and lakes.

Nunavut

The new territory of Nunavut (which means "our land") occupies an area of some 1.9 million sq km (0.73 million sq mi) and accounts for almost one-fifth of Canada's total land area. Much of the territory consists of islands stretching into the Arctic Ocean. The least populated of Canada's provinces and territories, Nunavut came into being in 1999 as a response to Inuit land claims in the Northwest Territories (of which it was formerly a part). The creation of Nunavut, whose capital is Iqaluit on Baffin Island, was the first major change to Canada's map since the incorporation of the province of Newfoundland (including Labrador) in 1949.

The terrain is characterized by mountains, rivers, and lakes. Geologically it is part of the Canadian Shield, with thin soil or bare rocky outcrops. Either permanent ice caps or Arctic tundra cover almost all of the land, apart from a small area in the southwest where marginal taiga forest grows. Mosses and dwarf shrubs are also found. The territory has rich mineral deposits, such as gold, lead, and zinc.

Saskatchewan

The central prairie province of Saskatchewan covers an area of 651,900 sq km (251,700 sq mi). The name comes from the Saskatchewan River, which means "swift flowing river" in the Cree language. It is one of only two completely landlocked Canadian provinces— the other being Alberta.

Saskatchewan has two major geographical regions: the northern third of the province forms part of the Canadian Shield; the remainder of the land consists of plains that drop from about 1,000 m (3,280 ft) above sea level in the west to 500 m (1,640 ft) in the east. Most of northern Saskatchewan is covered with boreal forest and features large lakes, such as Lake Athabasca and Lake Cree. In southwest Saskatchewan lie the Cypress Hills—an area that remained unglaciated during the last Ice Age. The highest point in the province, at 1,468 m (4,816 ft), is located in these hills.

A rural province, Saskatchewan's economy is based on agriculture, forestry, fishing, and trapping. The province grows about 45 percent of Canada's grain, mainly in the form of wheat, but also canola, oats,

barley, rye, flax, and other commodities. Saskatchewan produces large quantities of beef (of Canada's provinces, only Alberta produces more). Forestry is a significant activity in the north. The province also has an important industrial base and is the world's largest exporter of potash. It is also the world's most important supplier of uranium. Natural gas and oil production also play a significant part in Saskatchewan's economy. Other industries include chemicals and electrical equipment. The provincial capital is Regina, although the largest city in Saskatchewan is Saskatoon.

Located in southern Ontario, Algonquin Provincial Park is a 7,725-sq-km- (2,983-sq-mi-) area of forests, lakes, and rivers.

Manitoba

The most easterly of the Canadian prairie provinces, Manitoba covers an area of about 650,087 sq km (250,998 sq mi). The provincial capital is Winnipeg, located to the south of huge Lake Winnipeg (the world's 10th-largest freshwater lake), which dominates the south-central part of the province. Indeed, lakes of various sizes cover nearly 15 percent of Manitoba.

Manitoba has a long coastline on the shores of the Hudson Bay. Two-thirds of Manitoba (mainly the north and east) lies within the Canadian Shield area. The south-central part of Manitoba is fairly flat, but there are hilly regions, such as Baldy Mountain—the highest point at 832 m (2,727 ft) above sea level. Much of eastern, southeastern, and northern Manitoba is covered with pristine coniferous and birch forests, providing a haven for wildlife. Some of the world's best-preserved intact boreal forest is to be found along the eastern shores of Lake Winnipeg.

In the far north there is tundra. The climate is continental, with warm to hot summers and very cold winters. The prairies of the south produce crops such as wheat and oilseed, and cattle are reared for beef and dairy produce. Minerals include zinc, copper, uranium, and lead, and the chief industries are mining, food processing, and manufacturing.

Ontario

The second-largest Canadian province, Ontario covers an area of 1,068,582 sq km (412,580 sq mi). Most of the province's borders with the United States are natural features, beginning in the west at Lake of the Woods and continuing eastward through the four Great Lakes: Superior, Huron, Erie, and Ontario, then along the St. Lawrence River near Cornwall. Ontario's capital is Toronto, the largest city in Canada. Ottawa, Canada's capital, is also situated in Ontario. Ontario's population numbers about 12,687,000—approximately 39 percent of the country's total.

The province takes its name from Lake Ontario, which is thought to derive from *Onitariio* or *Skanadario*, meaning "beautiful water." Together with Nova Scotia, New Brunswick, and Quebec, Ontario was one of the four original provinces of Canada when the nation was formed in 1867 by the British North America Act.

Northern Ontario forms part of the rocky Canadian Shield. It is an area studded with lakes and forests and rich in minerals. The best-known geographic feature is Niagara Falls, part of the extensive Niagara Escarpment. The mild southwest is an important region for agriculture, producing wheat, corn, and soybean. It also produces most of the country's tobacco and much of its fruit and vegetables. Important minerals in the province include nickel, copper, lead, and uranium.

Ontario is Canada's leading manufacturing province, producing steel, automobiles, chemicals, and electrical goods. Its industrial base accounts for more than half the total annual manufactured exports. The province is ideally located for transporting goods to the heart of the United States, and the St. Lawrence Seaway allows navigation to and from the Atlantic Ocean as far inland as Thunder Bay in northwestern Ontario.

Quebec

Canada's largest province extends over an area of 1,358,000 sq km (524,300 sq mi) in the east of the country. Quebec encompasses three geographical regions: the Canadian Shield in the north, the St. Lawrence Lowland Valley (where most people live), and the plateaus of the Appalachian region, rising to 1,000 m (3,280 ft) near the U.S. border. Quebec's

capital is Quebec City, situated on the St. Lawrence Seaway. Farther south is Montreal, the most highly populated city in Quebec. Quebec's official language is French; it is the only Canadian province whose population is mainly French Canadian, and where English is not an official language at provincial level.

Southern and western Quebec have a continental climate with warm summers and cold winters; most of central Quebec is subarctic, while the north has Arctic conditions. The St. Lawrence Valley is a fertile region producing fruit, vegetables, maple syrup (Quebec is the world's biggest producer), dairy products, and livestock. Farther north the fur trade is important. Huge coniferous forests supply timber for pulp, paper, and lumber production, and hydroelectricity powers important industries, including those associated with the province's rich mineral supplies of nickel, copper, lead, and uranium. Quebec is a key player in the information and communication technologies as well as the aerospace, biotechnology, and health industries.

Newfoundland

Totaling some 372,000 sq km (143,634 sq mi), Canada's most easterly province consists of Labrador on the mainland and a triangular island at the mouth of the Gulf of St. Lawrence. Formerly a British colony, Newfoundland joined Canada in 1949. A large part of Newfoundland island is plateaulike, but it rises to the Long Range Mountains in the northeast. The island's coastline is heavily indented, as is that of Labrador. Off the coast there are numerous smaller islands. The provincial capital is St. John's. Historically, the Canadian fishing industry centered on Newfoundland. Today's catches are taken chiefly by large trawlers fishing the banks out to the extended 400-km- (250-mi-) limit set by the Canadian government in 1977.

Prince Edward Island

Canada's smallest province is a small, crescent-shaped island in the Gulf of St. Lawrence occupying an area of 5,660 sq km (2,185 sq mi). It is separated from the mainland by the Northumberland Strait. Prince Edward Island consists of lowlands rising to red sandstone cliffs. Two-thirds of the land is cultivated, with major crops including potatoes, tobacco, and vegetables. The island's attractive landscape of small farms, rolling hills, forests, and sandy beaches and coves, together with its

Toronto, Ontario's capital and Canada's largest city, lies on the north shore of Lake Ontario. To the left of this picture, the CN tower soars above the city skyline.

gentler pace of life, make it an important tourist location. The provincial capital is Charlottetown.

Nova Scotia

Nova Scotia, whose capital is Halifax, occupies a mainland peninsula in the east of the country and also includes Cape Breton Island and Sable Island. It covers a total area of 55,284 sq km (21,345 sq mi). The province's landscape is characterized by wooded hills and valleys, with numerous rivers and lakes and a picturesque coastline. The economy is primarily resource-based but has diversified in recent years. Fishing, mining, forestry, and agriculture remain significant, but tourism, technology, and industries such as filmmaking have grown in importance.

New Brunswick

This province of 73,436 sq km (28,354 sq mi) has a long coastline, bounded in the south by the Bay of Fundy, which has one of the widest tidal ranges in the world. Inland, the landscape is a mixture of lowlands and mountain ranges. Forests cover a large part of the land, with major urban centers concentrated in the south. The capital is Fredericton. New Brunswick has a modern service-based economy dominated by the finance, insurance, education, and tourism. The rural primary economy is based on forestry, mining, farming, and fishing. The most valuable crop is potatoes, while the most valuable fish catches are lobster and scallops.

UNITED STATES OF AMERICA

NATIONAL DATA – UNITED STATES OF AMERICA

Land area   9,161,923 sq km (3,537,438sq mi)

Climate		Temperatures		Annual
	Altitude m (ft)	January °C(°F)	July °C(°F)	precipitation mm (in)
Barrow	42 (13)	-27 (17)	5 (41)	107 (4.2)
San Francisco	5 (16)	9 (49)	17 (63)	500 (48.4)
New Orleans	9 (30)	11 (51)	28 (82)	1,572 (61.8)
Chicago	190 (623)	-6 (21)	23 (73)	910 (35.8)
Washington, DC	22 (72)	-1 (35)	27 (80)	981 (38.6)

Major physical features   highest point: Mount McKinley 6,194 m (20,320 ft); longest river: Mississippi-Missouri 6,020 km (3,740 mi); largest lake: Lake Superior (part) 83,270 sq km (32,150 sq mi)

Population   (2006 est.) 298,444,215

Form of government   federal multiparty republic with two legislative houses

Armed forces   army 595,946; navy 376,750; air force 347,400

Largest cities   New York (8,141,241); Los Angeles (3,945,097); Chicago (2,818,628); Houston (2,059,430); Phoenix (1,474,184); Philadelphia (1,426,259); San Diego (1,311,612); San Antonio (1,299,646); Dallas (1,222,053); San Jose (898,624); Detroit (858,803); Jacksonville (822,117); Indianapolis (770,634)

Official language   English

Ethnic composition   White 81.7%; Black 12.9%; Asian 4.2%; Amerindian and Alaska native 1%; Native Hawaiian and other Pacific islander 0.2%

Religious affiliations   Protestant 52%; Roman Catholic 24%; Mormon 2%; Jewish 1%; Muslim 1%; other 10%; none 10%

Currency   1 United States dollar (USD) = 100 cents

Gross domestic product   (2006 est.) U.S. $12.98 trillion

Gross domestic product per capita   (2006 est.) U.S. $43,500

Life expectancy at birth   male 75.02 yr; female 80.82 yr

Major resources   coal, copper, lead, molybdenum, phosphates, uranium, bauxite, gold, iron, mercury, nickel, potash, silver, tungsten, zinc, petroleum, natural gas, timber, fisheries, tourism, cereals, citrus fruits, cotton, fish, livestock, oilseeds, potatoes, soybeans, sugar beet, timber, tobacco, vegetables

The United States occupies a large part of the North American continent. As well as the 48 states bordered by Canada in the north and Mexico in the south (the coterminous states), the United States includes the states of Alaska on the northwestern tip of North America, Hawaii in the Pacific Ocean, and a number of island territories. It is the fourth-largest country in the world after Russia, Canada, and China, and it has the third-largest population after China and India. Yet it is the world's leading nation in terms of economic, political, military, and cultural influence.

Geography

The United States is a land of huge geographical diversity. In the east the Appalachian Mountains overlook the eastern Atlantic plains and the varied coastlines of the Atlantic Ocean

(characterized by a series of islands, notably Long Island in New York State). The Appalachians range was formed more than 225 million years ago and has been worn down over time by erosion. In the Southeast, in southern Florida, the Everglades forms a vast swampland covering 10,300 sq km (4,000 sq mi).

West of the Appalachians lie the interior plains, drained by the Mississippi River and its tributaries. At the river's mouth the channels and swamps form the bayou. To the north, straddling the border with Canada, are the Great Lakes, formed by glacial action thousands of years ago. They are the world's largest continuous body of fresh water. Farther west the land rises to form the Great Plains, bordered by the Rocky Mountains.

The Rocky Mountains form a backbone down the western flank of the United States, running from Alaska in the north to New Mexico in the south and including some of the country's highest peaks as well as many active volcanoes. West of the Rockies lies a region of basins and ranges formed by land movements along huge fault lines in the Earth's crust. Beyond, the ranges and lowlands give way to the Pacific coastal region.

New York's Brooklyn Bridge spanning the East River, looking toward the financial district of Lower Manhattan.

Among the coterminous states the northeastern and midwestern states experience hot summers and cold winters, whereas the subtropical Southeast enjoys mild winters. The southeastern coasts are subject to seasonal hurricanes, and tornadoes occur in states on the Gulf of Mexico. The Pacific coast as far south as San Francisco has a rainy climate, but winters are mild. This region, together with southeastern states, has over 1,000 mm (40 in) of rainfall each year. The mountains are cooler and wetter than the dry prairies to the east and desert basins, such as Death Valley, in the Southwest. California has a Mediterranean-style climate. The northwest is cooler and wetter. Alaska has polar and subarctic climates, while Hawaii has a subtropical climate moderated by cool trade winds.

Most of the original deciduous forest of the eastern states has long since been felled, but there are some stands of elm, beech, and maple. Conifers grow in the colder northern areas and on high ground. About halfway across the central basin the tree cover gives way to grassland, although much is now converted to agricultural land. Alpine vegetation covers the western mountains, with desert vegetation, such as cacti and succulents, in the arid areas in between. On the coasts of Oregon and California are Douglas firs and redwoods—at 90 m (300 ft) high, the world's tallest trees. Central and southern California has chaparral vegetation, with drought-resistant plants. Palm trees are native to parts of California and Florida.

UNITED STATES OF AMERICA

Society

America's first settlers probably arrived in Alaska from Siberia via the Bering Strait during the ice ages about 30,000 years ago. They spread rapidly, and their descendants developed a wide variety of societies and cultures. Their homes, for example, ranged from the cliff villages of the Pueblos in the Southwest to the bark lodges of the Iroquois in the northeast and the decorated wooden halls of the Northwest Coast Indians. It is possible that Vikings landed in the area around 1,000 A.D. Spanish and Portuguese explorers arrived in the 16th century.

The first English settlement was established in 1607, and the first of the New England colonies, Plymouth—founded by the Pilgrim Fathers—came in 1620. Other colonies followed, but resentment over laws imposed from Britain led to the 13 original colonies declaring their independence from Britain in 1776. A bloody war ensued, ending eventually in victory for the separatists, and George Washington was elected first president in 1789. By the mid-1800s the United States had expanded to more or less its present size. New lands had been added to the original colonies, and the nation stretched to the Pacific in the far west.

From 1861 to 1865 a Civil War was fought between the South, which supported slavery, and the North, which believed in freedom for all. The North won, and slavery was abolished. From the 1870s many Europeans settled in the United States, looking for a better life and helping fuel an expansion of American culture and economic and military might. In the 20th century the United States achieved worldwide cultural dominance and became the world's great superpower, marked by achievements such as pioneering medical advancements and historic landings on the Moon.

Economy

The United States has the world's largest economy, and its people enjoy the highest standard of living after the Japanese. But not all Americans benefit from this vast wealth. The country's economy is dominated by the industrial and business sectors. Although its agriculture is vast—about half the land area of the United States is used for agriculture—it plays only a small part in wealth

creation. Crops range from corn, sugar beet, cotton, fruit, sunflowers, vegetables, and groundnuts. Like crops, livestock production varies from area to area. The United States is also one of the five leading fishing nations in the world, although pollution is a major threat.

Immense natural resources are found in the United States, which is a leading producer of valuable metals such as copper, lead, silver, gold, and zinc. The nation also has one about one-third of the world's recoverable high-quality coal and one-eighth of its lignite. Yet despite these resources it cannot supply all the energy and raw materials demanded by its massive industrial output and adventurous foreign policy. Recent years have seen an increase in service industries at the

The stark, arid landscape of the American Southwest is exemplified here in Park Avenue at Arches National Park, Arizona.

expense of the traditional manufacturing sector. A decline in the industrial northeastern states has been offset by the rise of new industries and technologies in the south and southwest.

About 15 percent of the world's trade is handled by the United States—a higher volume than any other country. Canada is the country's leading trade partner, having overtaken Japan. Other major trading partners are Mexico, the EU, and China. The United States also exercises its influence over the rest of the world as the leading source of investment capital. Tourism brings significant revenue earnings, with visitors attracted to coastal and mountain resorts, major cities, national monuments and parks, and theme parks.

Transportation is modern and efficient. The national road system has the longest mileage of any in the world. The railroad network is also the world's largest, and it carries a significant amount of the nation's freight. Airlines cater to long-distance travel within the United States and internationally. The waterway network is also extensive. Despite the nation's wealth, poverty and racial issues affect many aspects of welfare provision, and about 10 percent of the population lives below the poverty line. Medical and educational facilities are good in most areas.

STATES OF THE UNITED STATES

The democratic governmental system of the United States was based on that of 18th-century Britain, but there are several differences. The federal government operates a system whereby the executive, legislative, and judicial branches are separate entities. The head of the executive branch is the president, whose tenure is restricted to a maximum of two terms (eight years) and who works with a cabinet whose members are not allowed to serve in the second tier of government, namely Congress. The latter consists of the 100-member Senate and the 435-member House of Representatives. Senators are elected for six-year terms, and there are two from each state, regardless of population or size. Representatives are elected for two-year terms, but from congressional districts of more equal sizes.

Of the two houses the Senate is the more powerful because its approval is required for the ratification of foreign treaties and for important appointments. The success of a president depends on the support of Congress as a whole, and new legislation must be supported not just by the president but by both houses of Congress before it can be approved. The third branch of the federal government is the judiciary, headed by the nine-judge Supreme Court, the main purpose of which is to interpret the civil rights enshrined in the American constitution.

In addition to the federal government, each state has its own constitution. Different states levy different rates of sales taxes, for example, and some impose the death penalty, while others do not. Many people believe that individual states should control more of their own affairs and object to central government's revenue-raising and spending powers.

States of the United States

- ■ national capital
- ● state capital

CONN.	CONNECTICUT
D.C.	DISTRICT OF COLUMBIA
DEL.	DELAWARE
MD.	MARYLAND
MASS.	MASSACHUSETTS
MISS.	MISSISSIPPI
N.J.	NEW JERSEY
R.I.	RHODE ISLAND
W. VA.	WEST VIRGINIA

ALABAMA

Nickname	Cotton State
Joined the Union	1819
Capital	Montgomery
Area	133,915 sq km (51,705 sq mi)
Population	4,599,030
Outstanding features	Cheaha Mountain, Mobile Bay
Principal industries	pulp and paper, chemicals, electronics

Alabama

The southeastern state of Alabama has a history distinguished by settlement disputes between European colonists and Native Americans, by issues of social reform in the 19th century, and by civil rights protests in the 1960s. Spain, France, and Britain all laid claim to the region, with France initiating the importation of African slaves. In 1763 the British gained control of most of the area. The Alabama Territory was created in 1817, achieving statehood in 1819.

By 1860 it was a wealthy cotton-growing state dependent on black labor—half the population of Alabama at that time were black slaves. (Today, the nickname for Alabama is the Cotton State.) Secession from the Union in 1861 was all but inevitable, and Alabama joined the Confederate States of America. After the Civil War—during which the state suffered huge casualties—a period of reconstruction merely deepened the gulf between blacks and whites and created increasing support for the white supremacist creed of the Ku Klux Klan. Basic civil rights for blacks came only after years of protest during the 1950s and 1960s. The protests included the march on Montgomery, the capital, by the black American civil rights leader Martin Luther King (1929-68) in 1965.

Agriculture remains an important industry today, with cotton and groundnuts (peanuts) among the chief crops grown. Manufacturing has diversified from iron and steel and agriculture-based industries to include textiles and modern electronics. Resources in the state include coal, oil, and natural gas. Montgomery is situated about 220 km (135 mi) from the Gulf of Mexico and is a business and market center.

The southern Alaskan town of Homer. Alaska is the largest state and was the penultimate one to join the Union.

ALASKA

Nickname	The Last Frontier
Joined the Union	1959
Capital	Juneau
Area	1,530,693 sq km (591,004 sq mi)
Population	670,053
Outstanding features	Mount McKinley, Glacier Bay National Park
Principal industries	gas and petroleum mining, tourism, fishing

Alaska

Alaska is situated in the far northwest of North America, with Canada to the east and the Bering Strait, which separates it from Russia, to the west. The southernmost part of Alaska is called the Panhandle; it is a narrow strip of land running south along the northern Pacific coast, bordering Canada inland. The coast along the Gulf of Alaska is lined by an almost continuous mountain chain characterized by glaciers, volcanoes, and severe earthquakes. North of the Alaska Range is the broad central plateau, greatly fragmented by the Yukon River and its tributaries. North of here, the Brooks Range runs right across the state; and northward again a broad coastal plain, covered by tundra, borders the Atlantic Ocean. Alaska was bought from Tsarist Russia in 1867.

The discovery of gold in the late 19th and 20th centuries led to huge increases in population as prospectors headed for the cold remote lands in search of fortune. Today, industries include natural gas and petroleum exploitation, forestry, fishing, and tourism. The southern mountains of the Alaska Range contain the highest peak in the United States, Mount McKinley (6,194 m/20,320 ft). The climate is generally cold, with the greatest extremes of temperature found in the drier areas of the interior and the north.

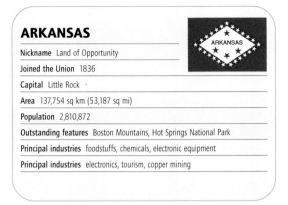

ARKANSAS

Nickname Land of Opportunity

Joined the Union 1836

Capital Little Rock ·

Area 137,754 sq km (53,187 sq mi)

Population 2,810,872

Outstanding features Boston Mountains, Hot Springs National Park

Principal industries foodstuffs, chemicals, electronic equipment

Principal industries electronics, tourism, copper mining

ARIZONA

Nickname Grand Canyon State

Joined the Union 1912

Capital Phoenix

Area 295,259 sq km (114,000 sq mi)

Population 6,166,318

Outstanding features Grand Canyon, Painted Desert, Petrified Forest National Park

Principal industries electronics, tourism, copper mining

Arkansas

On the west bank of the Mississippi River, Arkansas extends westward to the forested uplands of the Ozark Plateau and Ouachita Mountains. Native American cultures were established in the area by 500 A.D. French settlers who arrived in the 17th century sold the territory to the United States in the Louisiana Purchase of 1803. The lower Mississippi plains became the site of great cotton plantations worked by black slaves from Africa. From 1820 until 1836, when statehood was granted, Arkansaw Territory was the area south of the Missouri Compromise line, which separated slave and free states. The state was impoverished after the Civil War and overly dependent on cotton. Today the state is much more prosperous, but largely rural. New industries, including tourism, have replaced cotton.

Arizona

Arizona is one of America's youngest states, but one that has been inhabited the longest. Native American peoples flourished in this area for at least 25,000 years. The Spanish took the region, and it remained in their control until 1848, when it was ceded to the United States; further territory was added by the Gadsden Purchase of 1853. Many legends of the Wild West are rooted in Arizona; Tombstone, for example, was the site of the notorious gunfight at the OK Corral.

During the 1970s Arizona's population was nearly doubled by immigrants from other states, attracted by the sunny climate and employment opportunities in cities such as Tucson and Phoenix. Yet most areas are sparsely populated. Native Americans are more numerous here than in many other states, but they are heavily outnumbered by Spanish speakers. Arizona's spectacular scenery, with mountains rising above plains, is a major asset, and it has a thriving tourist industry.

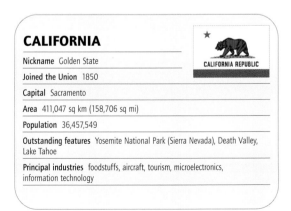

CALIFORNIA

Nickname Golden State

Joined the Union 1850

Capital Sacramento

Area 411,047 sq km (158,706 sq mi)

Population 36,457,549

Outstanding features Yosemite National Park (Sierra Nevada), Death Valley, Lake Tahoe

Principal industries foodstuffs, aircraft, tourism, microelectronics, information technology

California

The most populated state, with an economy the size of many large nations, California has the world's heaviest concentration of motor vehicles and a huge freeway system. The San Andreas Fault runs the length of the state from Cape Mendocino in the north to north of San Francisco, making the area vulnerable to earthquakes.

The first official Spanish expedition to the region arrived in 1769, although the coast had been seen much earlier—in 1542 by Juan Rodríguez Cabrillo (d. 1543). In the same year a Franciscan mission was set up at Monterey, on the coast. In 1821 Mexico gained independence from Spain, and soon Mexican settlers had taken over the mission ranches, expelling the Native American population. The area had also attracted white American settlers, and in 1848, after a war with Mexico, the territory was ceded to the United States. The discovery of gold east of Sacramento heralded a further influx of settlers.

Today California is a prime agricultural state. It also has large reserves of petroleum and thriving business and industrial sectors as well as massive income from tourism. Silicon Valley has become famous in the field of information technology. Hollywood, near Los Angeles, is the world's film and television capital.

Reminders of a Spanish colonial past, traditional-style buildings nestle beneath modern high-rise blocks in San Francisco, California.

COLORADO

Nickname Centennial State

Joined the Union 1876

Capital Denver

Area 269,594 sq km (104,091 sq mi)

Population 4,753,377

Outstanding features Mount Elbert (Rocky Mountains), Black Canyon, Garden of the Gods

Principal industries microelectronics, foodstuffs, machinery

Colorado

Colorado, lying astride the Rockies, is the archetypal Western state. It was home to various Native Americans, ranging from the Mesa Verde cliff dwellers to Plains peoples such as the Cheyenne and Arapaho. They were later overrun by the Spanish, who named the area Colorado ("red," or "ruddy") after the reddish color of its rocks. The eastern side, annexed by France, was sold in the Louisiana Purchase in 1803; the west passed from Mexico to the United States in 1848. The 1859 gold rush brought an influx of settlers, creating many frontier towns. Their need for food stimulated the development of irrigated agriculture, and cattle and

sheep farming replaced the exterminated buffalo herds. In the late 19th century the discovery of rich mineral reserves made the new state a major industrial sector.

In recent years Colorado's older industries have suffered setbacks, but they have to a certain extent been replaced by modern computer and aerospace industries. The awesome beauty of the Rockies and the ideal skiing conditions of resorts such as Aspen support an ever-expanding tourist industry.

CONNECTICUT

Nickname	Constitution State
Ratified the Constitution	1788
Capital	Hartford
Area	12,997 sq km (5,018 sq mi)
Population	3,504,809
Outstanding features	Connecticut River, Long Island Sound
Principal industries	military equipment, insurance, electrical equipment

---

Connecticut

Lying on the New England coast between the cities of Boston and New York, Connecticut is one of the oldest and proudest communities in the United States. The colony was founded in the 1630s by Puritans—originally from Britain—who had left Massachusetts Bay Colony. The colonists got on well with the local Algonquin peoples and settled in the Connecticut River Valley and the coastal strip beyond Saybrook and New Haven. In 1662 a royal charter provided effective self-government. More than half the army under the command of George Washington (1732–99) In 1776 was drawn from Connecticut. A stream of Irish immigrants began in the 1840s, swelled later by French Canadian and European immigrants.

Textile factories began to displace agriculture as the main source of employment. Farming is only a small part of the economy today. Some original 19th-century industries—such as clock- and gun-making—remain, but the economy is now more service based. Although there are no large cities, most people are urban dwellers. Local autonomy is prized, and local history is preserved in many forms.

Yale University, Connecticut. One of America's most renowned seats of learning, Yale was established in 1761, initially as Yale College.

DELAWARE

Nickname	First State
Ratified the Constitution	1787
Capital	Dover
Area	5,294 sq km (2,044 sq mi)
Population	853,476
Outstanding features	Delaware River, Delaware Bay
Principal industries	chemicals, textiles, clothing

DECEMBER 7, 1787

Delaware

Delaware is heavily industrialized and densely populated. The north of the state forms part of the Atlantic megapolis—the long urban corridor running from Washington, DC, to Boston. Dutch settlers reclaimed the area from Native Americans but lost it to the British in 1664. Delaware gained its own assembly in 1704 and its present name in 1776. After independence, Delaware's prompt acceptance of the Constitution of December 7, 1787, earned it the title of the First State.

The development of industry has had a marked effect on the demographic balance of the state. The older rural communities around Dover and Georgetown in the mainly agricultural south have now declined. Extensive suburban areas have grown up in the industrial north, especially around Wilmington, which is now a major center for artificial fibers.

FLORIDA

Nickname Sunshine State

Joined the Union 1845

Capital Tallahassee

Area 151,939 sq km (58,664 sq mi)

Population 18,089,888

Outstanding features the Everglades, Florida Keys

Principal industries tourism, electronics, electrical machinery, foodstuffs

Florida

Florida's early history is one marked by persecution of the local Native American population by Spanish colonists and the destruction in 1565 of a Huguenot settlement. For 200 years control of Florida was disputed between Great Britain, France, and Spain, but the British finally took control. During the War of Independence Florida remained loyal to Britain. It was seized by Spain in 1781 but was ceded to the United States in 1819.

After the Civil War new railroads brought settlers and tourists, beginning a period of rapid expansion in population that continued through the 20th century. Many elderly people retire to Florida from northern cities, and after the 1959 Cuban revolution many Cuban refugees settled in the state, especially in Miami.

Much of the land is forested, and there are lakes and reserves. Although there are extensive citrus fruit plantations, tourism is the leading industry, with many visitors to the Everglades National Park in the south

and to Disney World near Orlando in central Florida. The state also hosts many major sporting events, including football, golf, and auto racing. The Kennedy Space Center at Cape Canaveral also makes a significant contribution to the economy, as does the production of electrical machinery.

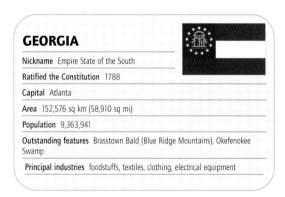

GEORGIA

Nickname Empire State of the South

Ratified the Constitution 1788

Capital Atlanta

Area 152,576 sq km (58,910 sq mi)

Population 9,363,941

Outstanding features Brasstown Bald (Blue Ridge Mountains), Okefenokee Swamp

Principal industries foodstuffs, textiles, clothing, electrical equipment

Georgia

In 1732 George II of England (1683–1760) granted a charter for the formation of a new colony in North America. Georgia, the last of the 13 original colonies, was founded to give opportunities in a new land to some of Britain's poorest citizens. In 1752 the colony reverted to crown control, however. Other settlers then arrived before the War of Independence. Later, they came in such numbers that they displaced the original Native American inhabitants beyond the Mississippi River. Black slaves were subsequently brought in to work the state's developing cotton plantations.

The issue of slavery caused much heart searching in Georgia, but in 1861 the state convention voted for secession from the Union. The result of this was devastation for the state in the Civil War, and the capture of the president of the Confederacy, Jefferson Davis (1808–89), on Georgian soil. Georgia's politicians resisted black enfranchisement for another century, and it was a hotly debated issue until as late as 1967.

Cotton is no longer the main crop, having been overtaken by groundnuts and corn. Textiles remain important, together with many new industries, such as electronics. Federal military installations supplement income from industry. Atlanta is the national headquarters of the Coca-Cola Company, and its rapid growth in recent years makes it the commercial and financial center of the Southeast as well as a leading national city. Atlanta hosted the 1996 Olympic Games.

HAWAII

Nickname Aloha State	
Joined the Union 1959	
Capital Honolulu	
Area 16,760 sq km (6,471 sq mi)	
Population 1,285,498	
Outstanding features Mauna Kea (the world's highest island peak), Mauna Loa	
Principal industries tourism, foodstuffs, defense industries	

Hawaii

Hawaii comprises a chain of steep, volcanic Pacific islands about 3,800 km (2,400 mi) southwest of the Californian coast. The state is named for the largest island. The islands were first settled by Polynesians, but they came under U.S. protection in 1851. American influence grew, until in 1900 the islands were annexed to the United States. A huge naval base was built at Pearl Harbor, and in 1941 this was attacked by Japan, bringing the United States into World War II. Hawaii was by now so firmly American in character that

The capital of Hawaii, Honolulu, viewed from Diamond Head Crater. Hawaii is America's most far-flung state, and its newest.

incorporation as the 50th state was inevitable. Hawaii supports several industries, notably sugar refining, but its greatest asset is its natural beauty. The climate is mild, and lush forests cover the slopes of the volcanic mountains, many of which are active. Clear air and cloudless skies make their upper slopes an ideal site for astronomical observatories. Not surprisingly, the islands are a great tourist attraction, giving millions of mainland Americans each year a taste of Polynesia.

IDAHO

Nickname Gem State	
Joined the Union 1890	
Capital Boise	
Area 216,430 sq km (83,564 sq mi)	
Population 1,466,465	
Outstanding features Hell's Canyon, Craters of the Moon National Monument, Shoshone Falls	
Principal industries foodstuffs, timber processing, chemicals	

Idaho

Idaho lies in the northwest of the United States, its short northern frontier touching the Canadian border. Its center is dominated by several of the Rocky Mountain ranges, and the south by the lava landscapes of the Snakes River Plain. Native Americans such as the Shoshoni had lived here as hunter-gatherers for at least 10,000 years; their descendants still inhabit the area.

Idaho was originally part of Oregon Country, and it was obtained by treaty from Britain in 1846. It was first settled by gold prospectors and then by Confederate refugees after the Civil War. Many Mormons also settled here, fleeing persecution for their religion in the east. They did much to build up the state and still form the majority in the Southeast. Idaho has a small but growing manufacturing base, including chemicals, but the state still depends on a strongly agricultural economy. It is famous for its vast potato crop, its wheat fields, and its lumber.

ILLINOIS

Nickname Prairie State

Joined the Union 1818

Capital Springfield

Area 149,885 sq km (57,871 sq mi)

Population 12,831,970

Outstanding features Illinois and Mississippi Rivers

Principal industries fabricated metals, electrical machinery, electronics, chemicals

Illinois

illinois is a state of great contrasts: urban Chicago on the shores of Lake Michigan on the one hand, and the agricultural lands of the prairies to the south and west on the other. French explorers arrived in 1673 and established settlements along the Illinois River. The area was ceded to Britain in 1763, but this caused disruption to the Native Americans' way of life, and subsequent conflict. The area passed to America during the War of Independence, and Chicago was founded by the black pioneer merchant Jean-Baptiste-Point Du Sable (1750–1818) in about 1790. The Illinois Territory was created in 1809, followed by a wave of settlement. The Black Hawk War of 1832 ended conflict with the Native Americans, and slavery was abolished in 1848.

Chicago prospered after the Civil War thanks to massive industrial expansion, and immigrants from Europe flocked to work there. During the Prohibition era of the 1920s and 1930s, rivalry between bootleg gangs made the city a byword for violence,

overshadowing its significant social and cultural achievements. Meanwhile, the agricultural south shared some of the antiblack violence of the Ku Klux Klan. The distinction between north and south Illinois is still strong. Agriculture is important, but industry, trade, insurance, and transportation are the major contributors to the state income. Chicago's O'Hare International Airport is one of the busiest in the world.

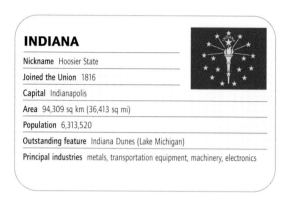

INDIANA

Nickname Hoosier State

Joined the Union 1816

Capital Indianapolis

Area 94,309 sq km (36,413 sq mi)

Population 6,313,520

Outstanding feature Indiana Dunes (Lake Michigan)

Principal industries metals, transportation equipment, machinery, electronics

Indiana

Indiana straddles the Midwest from Lake Michigan to the Ohio River and shares many characteristics of both northern and southern states. The land consists mostly of rolling plains covered in fertile glacial soils. The original inhabitants of the region were the Algonquin who, to protect their land against incursions from the hostile Iroquois peoples, formed what was called the Miami Confederation. The first European settlers were French, but the area passed to Britain and was ceded to the United States in 1783. Homesteaders from the east then rapidly moved in to open up its fertile land for farming, as improved transportation links made access possible. The Civil War brought industrialization to the north and an influx of refugees from the south, who strongly influenced the state's social and political character; they brought with them slavery and a strong distrust of federal government.

Modern Indiana is predominantly an industrial state. Its transportation network is highly developed, including the Ohio River, which is used to carry freight at low costs. Railroad and road density are higher than the national average. Much of Indiana is still relatively unspoiled, especially in the agricultural south.

IOWA

Nickname	Hawkeye State
Joined the Union	1846
Capital	Des Moines
Area	145,752 sq km (56,275 sq mi)
Population	2,982,085
Outstanding features	Okoboji Lakes, Effigy Mounds National Monument
Principal industries	foodstuffs, agricultural machinery, electronics

Iowa

The Midwestern state of Iowa lies between the Mississippi and Missouri Rivers at the very heart of the North American continent. It is bordered by Minnesota to the north, Nebraska and South Dakota to the west, Missouri to the south, and Wisconsin and Illinois to the east. Ice-age glaciers once scoured its landscape but left rich soils behind them. The topography of the state consists of gently rolling plains., with hills along the western border. Some of these are several hundred feet thick. In the northeast, along the Mississippi River, is a section of the Driftless Zone, which in Iowa consists of low hills clad with conifers—a landscape not usually associated with this state.

The original inhabitants of the area were Sioux and other Native American peoples, whose Plains cultures reached their height after the horse had been introduced from Europe. The area was first claimed by the French, but was part of the vast Louisiana colony purchased by the United States in 1803, opening the way for settlers from the east and later from central Europe; the German and Czech communities retain much of their traditional identity today.

Iowa is nowadays an almost exclusively agricultural state, producing a vast amount of livestock—especially pigs and cattle—and feed crops annually. It is by no means a backwater, however, with modern cities such as Des Moines, the capital, and Sioux City. The state also boasts prestigious educational institutions such as the University of Iowa in Iowa City. Des Moines stands in the middle of the state on the Des Moines River, about 190 km (120 mi) east of the Missouri River. The city is a trade, manufacturing, and cultural center.

The state of Iowa is mainly agricultural and dotted with farms and small villages. Windmills pump up water in the flat landscape.

KANSAS

Nickname	Sunflower State
Joined the Union	1861
Capital	Topeka
Area	213,096 sq km (82,277 sq mi)
Population	2,764,075
Outstanding features	Castle Rock, Horse Thief Canyon
Principal industries	foodstuffs, aircraft, agricultural machinery

Kansas

Kansas lies at the geographical heart of the United States. At the time of the dinosaurs it was the bed of a shallow inland sea, and its landscape remains mainly level today. Until Europeans arrived, Native Americans hunted the vast buffalo herds, but by the 1850s these had largely been exterminated, both to starve the Native Americans and to export the buffalo hides. The state was part of the area bought in the Louisiana Purchase of 1803, and later became a battleground over the slavery issue. At first the state relied largely

Cherokee. After 1767 it was explored by the frontiersman Daniel Boone (1734-1820), who paved the way for the westward migration of settlers. A substantial black slave population was imported into Kentucky, and the state government opposed the abolition of slavery. However, Kentucky did not join the Confederacy, and most of its soldiers fought for the Union in the Civil War. In the upland "hillbilly" country—poor and fiercely clannish—Civil War feuds continued into the 20th century.

Modern Kentucky has remained agricultural and is famous for its tobacco, horse breeding, and bourbon whiskey. Since the late 19th century, however, massive coal reserves have been exploited, and large areas have been laid waste by strip mining—although this practice has been controlled since 1966. Kentucky is also well known for its rich cultural heritage, ranging from the famous Kentucky Derby to folk music, including the celebrated Bluegrass style.

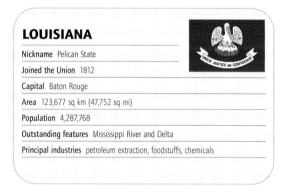

LOUISIANA

Nickname	Pelican State
Joined the Union	1812
Capital	Baton Rouge
Area	123,677 sq km (47,752 sq mi)
Population	4,287,768
Outstanding features	Mississippi River and Delta
Principal industries	petroleum extraction, foodstuffs, chemicals

on cattle, but hardy wheat strains opened up the vast wheat fields—although many were to become the overfarmed "dustbowls" of the 1930s. Kansas nonetheless remains the leading wheat state and a major meat producer. Industry is important, but is largely agriculturally based.

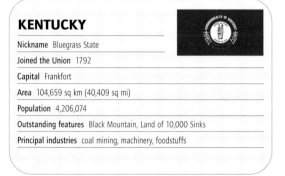

KENTUCKY

Nickname	Bluegrass State
Joined the Union	1792
Capital	Frankfort
Area	104,659 sq km (40,409 sq mi)
Population	4,206,074
Outstanding features	Black Mountain, Land of 10,000 Sinks
Principal industries	coal mining, machinery, foodstuffs

Kentucky

The south-central state of Kentucky lies between the Cumberland Mountains in the Southeast and the Ohio River to the north. Kentucky unites the traditions of the frontier and the old South with a modern industrial economy. The area was once the hunting ground of Native American peoples such as the Iroquois and the

Louisiana

Native Americans had been living in the area for 16,000 years before France claimed it in 1682. In 1718 New Orleans was founded near the Mississippi Delta, and in 1731 the crown colony of Louisiana was born. Many settlers arrived, including Cajuns—French-speakers expelled from Nova Scotia by the British. Louisiana fell into Spanish hands in 1762. The effect of this French and Spanish heritage is seen in the state's legal code and in its architecture and culture. In 1803 the United States acquired Louisiana as part of the Louisiana Purchase. As in other southern states, the cotton and sugarcane planters depended for their wealth on black slaves. Conflicts of interest soon occurred between wealthy planters and farmers over issues of land use and political suffrage. Louisiana seceded from the Union in 1861 but was readmitted in 1868. Blacks were denied voting rights until the civil rights campaigns of the 1960s.

Modern Louisiana remains primarily agricultural, but cotton is no longer the main crop, having given way to soybeans, rice, and other food crops. Beef cattle are also important. New Orleans was among the many places devastated by hurricane Katrina in 2005. It caused many deaths, wrecked the city's infrastructure and tourist industry, and left many people homeless.

MAINE	
Nickname Pine Tree State	
Joined the Union 1820	
Capital Augusta	
Area 86,156 sq km (33,265 sq mi)	
Population 1,321,574	
Outstanding features Mount Katahdin, Moosehead Lake	
Principal industries forestry, fisheries, paper	

Maine

Maine, the most northeasterly state in the United States, lies on the Atlantic seaboard of New England next to the border with Canada. It borders just one other U.S. state: New Hampshire. Much of the state is mountainous, with the highest point being Mount Katahdin in the east, which rises to 1,605 m (5,267 ft) above sea level. There are also many lakes, for example, Moosehead Lake. Forests cover much of the land area, giving rise to the state's nickname of Pine Tree State.

Maine's craggy coastline may have witnessed North America's first—albeit temporary—European visitors: 10th-century Vikings from Greenland. From the 15th century onward the area was disputed by both England and France, whose settlers met with fierce resistance from local Penobscot and Passamaquoddy peoples. The British finally prevailed in 1763, but the area belonged to Massachusetts until the war of 1812. It became a free state under

the 1820 Missouri Compromise as a balance to Missouri's status as a slave state.

Maine's stony, heavily forested landscape restricted agricultural development. Potatoes are still the main crop. However, as transportation improved during the 19th century, the rich resources of timber, stone, and fish formed the basis for important industries. Cheap water power attracted others. Today Maine is not especially prosperous by New England standards, but its natural beauty remains relatively unspoiled, to the benefit of its flourishing tourist industry. Camping, hiking, sailing, fishing, and hunting are among the outdoor attractions offered by the state.

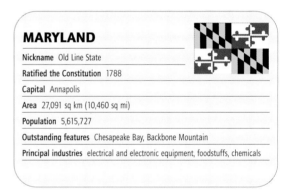

MARYLAND	
Nickname Old Line State	
Ratified the Constitution 1788	
Capital Annapolis	
Area 27,091 sq km (10,460 sq mi)	
Population 5,615,727	
Outstanding features Chesapeake Bay, Backbone Mountain	
Principal industries electrical and electronic equipment, foodstuffs, chemicals	

Maryland

The east coast state of Maryland straddles Chesapeake Bay and extends northwestward to the Appalachian Mountains. The British first settled the area in the 1600s, providing a haven for Roman Catholics suffering persecution in England. The first capital, St. Mary's City, was founded in 1634, but the rapid growth of tobacco plantations shifted the population centers to the northwest, and the capital moved to Annapolis. Baltimore, the largest city, was founded in 1729.

The state was active in the War of Independence; the 1783 Treaty of Paris, which acknowledged the independence of the colonies, was ratified in Annapolis. Maryland had divided loyalties in the Civil War, but the state remained with the Union. Baltimore is one of the nation's busiest ports, supported by a strong industrial base, including many new industries. Service industries are increasingly important, and the state's historical sites form the basis for a thriving tourist industry.

Historic Park Street Church contrasts with the modern, high-rise cityscape of Boston, the state capital of Massachusetts.

state saw many important battles during the ensuing War of Independence. Massachusetts became industrialized in the 19th century, and immigrants swelled the labor force. The Abolitionist movement also became strong here, and the state sided firmly with the Union in the Civil War. Its traditional industrial base in textiles has declined in recent decades, but the gap has been filled by new "hi-tech" industries, often stimulated by the presence of famous academic institutions such as Harvard and Boston Universities and the Massachusetts Institute of Technology (MIT).

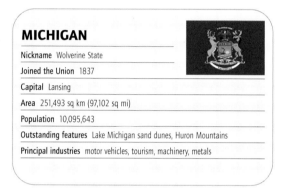

MICHIGAN

Nickname Wolverine State	
Joined the Union 1837	
Capital Lansing	
Area 251,493 sq km (97,102 sq mi)	
Population 10,095,643	
Outstanding features Lake Michigan sand dunes, Huron Mountains	
Principal industries motor vehicles, tourism, machinery, metals	

MASSACHUSETTS

Nickname Bay State	
Ratified the Constitution 1788	
Capital Boston	
Area 21,455 sq km (8,284 sq mi)	
Population 6,437,193	
Outstanding features Cape Cod, Martha's Vineyard (island)	
Principal industries electrical machinery, electronics, precision instruments	

Massachusetts

Massachusetts has a long and illustrious past, reflected in many historic sites and monuments. Vikings are thought to have landed in about 1003, long before the first European settlers arrived in any numbers. In 1620 a party of religious dissidents from England arrived by their ship the *Mayflower* to their new settlement, Plymouth. Relations with the local Native Americans were good initially but later turned to mutual hostility.

Massachusetts relied from earliest times on trade and industry rather than agriculture, and local resentment of British trade restraints made the colony a leader in the independence movement, provoking incidents such as the Boston Tea Party (1773). The

Michigan

Michigan occupies two great promontories surrounded by the Great Lakes. The state is associated with the U.S. automobile industry, but it also has extensive wild forest in the north and shares the rolling, fertile landscape of the Midwestern grain states that lie to the south. The area was originally inhabited by Native American peoples such as the Ottawa, but French fur traders and missionaries arrived in the 17th century. The area passed to Britain in 1760 and became its power base until the end of the War of Independence.

Industry grew apace, encouraged by substantial ore reserves, good transportation links, and plentiful labor. Detroit's prosperity vanished in the Great Depression of the 1930s but recovered after World War II. Michigan's industries are still suffering from economic recession, aggravated by a decline in the U.S. automobile industry. Tensions involving the large black population led to riots in the 1940s and 1960s, while Motown music, which originated as a distinct cultural form among black communities, soared to international popularity. Pollution, especially in the Great Lakes, has damaged the state's lakeside tourist industry.

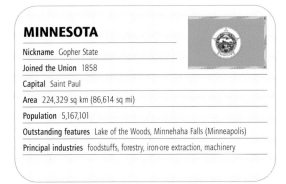

MINNESOTA

Nickname Gopher State
Joined the Union 1858
Capital Saint Paul
Area 224,329 sq km (86,614 sq mi)
Population 5,167,101
Outstanding features Lake of the Woods, Minnehaha Falls (Minneapolis)
Principal industries foodstuffs, forestry, iron-ore extraction, machinery

Minnesota

Minnesota borders North and South Dakota to the west, Iowa to the south, Wisconsin to the east, and Manitoba and Ontario in Canada to the north. The landscape was once scoured by glaciers, which left it dotted with many thousands of lakes, and covered its rolling prairies with fertile soils. Originally inhabited by the Chippewa and Sioux peoples and then by French fur traders, the area was acquired by the United States in the Louisiana Purchase of 1803. Settlers from New England, attracted by the wealth of the immense hardwood forests, began to arrive in the 1820s. The two urban settlements on either side of the Mississippi River were to grow into the so-called Twin Cities of Minneapolis and Saint Paul.

Later immigrants, some from Scandinavia and Germany, farmed the rich prairies, and iron-ore mines in the northeast formed the basis for industrial growth. Minnesota produces more than half of the country's iron ore. In the 20th century new large-scale farming methods opened up the grainfields upon which Minnesota's prosperity is now founded.

Trade and manufacturing are concentrated in Minneapolis and Saint Paul, each of which is also home to cultural and tourist centers. Despite being an inland state, the Great Lakes port of Duluth on Lake Superior gives Minnesota access to the sea.

MISSISSIPPI

Nickname Magnolia State
Joined the Union 1817
Capital Jackson
Area 123,514 sq km (47,689 sq mi)
Population 2,910,540
Outstanding feature Mississippi River
Principal industries clothing, foodstuffs, timber processing

Mississippi

The first colonists in the area were French Canadians. Other French settlers followed, but in 1763 the British took control. Spain then occupied the south during the War of Independence, and the area remained in dispute until 1795, when it was ceded to the United States. In 1817 the western part of the Mississippi Territory, which extended from Tennessee in the north to the Gulf coast in the south, became the state of Mississippi.

Native Americans were forcibly removed and, thanks to slavery, Mississippi became a prosperous cotton state. Entrenched attitudes to slavery led to its secession from the Union in 1861. It was devastated by the ensuing Civil War. By 1890 its black population was still virtually disenfranchised, and despite the civil

A pleasure boat, reminiscent of an old Mississippi paddle steamer, plies its trade.

rights legislation of the 1960s, the subsequent process of racial integration has been long and arduous. Agriculture was hit in the Great Depression of the 1930s, and, although it recovered after World War II, the state remains relatively backward economically, and industrial development has been lacking.

MISSOURI

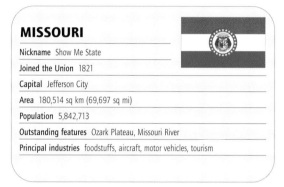

Nickname Show Me State	
Joined the Union 1821	
Capital Jefferson City	
Area 180,514 sq km (69,697 sq mi)	
Population 5,842,713	
Outstanding features Ozark Plateau, Missouri River	
Principal industries foodstuffs, aircraft, motor vehicles, tourism	

Missouri

Missouri borders Kansas to the west, Arkansas to the south, Illinois to the east, and Iowa to the north. It marks the divide between timberland and prairie, cornfields and cotton fields, slave owners and Abolitionists, east and west, and north and south.

Missouri's first European settlement, Sainte Genevieve, was established by French hunters and lead miners in the 1730s. In 1803 the area was acquired by the United States as part of the Louisiana Purchase, and American settlers moved in.

Despite being a slave state, Missouri joined the Union in 1821 following the introduction, by Congress, of the controversial Missouri Compromise, the ostensible purpose of which was to regulate the spread of slavery to western territories. The "compromise" was that the overall status quo would be preserved by the simultaneous admission to the Union of Maine, a nonslave state. Missouri stayed within the Union during the Civil War, but many Missourians fought on the Confederate side. After the Civil War lawlessness and banditry continued, much of it led by the likes of Jesse and Frank James (1847–82 and 1843–1914). Although slavery was abolished in 1865, racial discrimination remained strong until well into the 1960s.

MONTANA

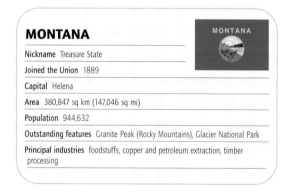

Nickname Treasure State	
Joined the Union 1889	
Capital Helena	
Area 380,847 sq km (147,046 sq mi)	
Population 944,632	
Outstanding features Granite Peak (Rocky Mountains), Glacier National Park	
Principal industries foodstuffs, copper and petroleum extraction, timber processing	

Montana

Acquired in the Louisiana Purchase of 1803, the area was not exploited until gold was discovered in the northern Rockies in 1862. This attracted a wave of prospectors. Two years later Montana Territory was created, and the first cattle ranchers moved in.

Native Americans fought hard to defend their traditional hunting grounds, and names such as Sioux and Cheyenne have become legendary, as have the battlefields where they won their last victories—Little Bighorn (1876) and the Bighole Basin (1877). Soon afterward, U.S. troops defeated the indigenous population, opening the way for white settlement.

Existing settlers soon turned their attention from gold to the massive copper deposits, while offers of free land brought immigrant homesteaders from northern Europe from 1909 onward. Mining and agriculture remain important to the economy, and many tourists are attracted by the dramatic scenery and history.

NEBRASKA

Nickname	Cornhusker State
Joined the Union	1867
Capital	Lincoln
Area	200,349 sq km (77,355 sq mi)
Population	1,768,331
Outstanding features	Platte and Missouri Rivers
Principal industries	foodstuffs, machinery, electronics

Nebraska

Nebraska is a major agricultural state, lying at the heart of the prairies. Originally exploited by French fur traders, the area was ceded to Spain in 1763, receded to France in 1801, acquired by the United States in 1803 as part of the Louisiana Purchase, and explored by Meriwether Lewis (1774-1807) and George Rogers Clark (1752-1818) from 1804 to 1806.

The fur trade continued to thrive, and by the 1840s the Platte Valley had become a gateway to the west for thousands of pioneers. Nebraska's agricultural potential led to the completion, in 1869, of the Union Pacific Railroad. As the settler population grew, so did Native American resistance.

Nebraska's farm economy became depressed in the 1890s, boomed once more in the early 20th century, only to decline during the Great Depression—and the dustbowl years—of the 1930s. World War II saw an upsurge in the economy with the arrival of military airfields and war industries.

Today, agriculture remains the dominant activity in the state, supplying raw materials for industries such as food processing and chemicals. The Platte Valley retains its historic importance as a major artery for trade, transportation, and communication links between east and west.

NEVADA

Nickname	Silver State
Joined the Union	1864
Capital	Carson City
Area	286,352 sq km (110,561 sq mi)
Population	2,495,529
Outstanding features	Boundary Peak, Carson Sink, Lake Mead (Boulder Canyon)
Principal industries	tourism, gold and mineral extraction, electronics, chemicals

Nevada

Nevada is a state of contrasts, ranging from the natural splendor of the Mojave Desert and the Sierra Nevada mountains (for which it is named), to the glitz of Las Vegas, one of the fastest-growing cities in the country. Native Americans have lived in the area for more than 20,000 years. The first European settlers were Spanish missionaries and Canadian fur traders in the 18th and

Las Vegas, a vibrant city of casinos and entertainment set in the Nevada Desert, is one of the country's biggest tourist destinations.

early 19th centuries. American explorers soon followed, opening up the west. In 1848 the area was ceded by Mexico to the United States. The 1859 Comstock Lode discovery caused a silver rush and attracted prospectors in great numbers. When monetary reforms caused a slump in the silver industry, people turned their attention to cattle ranching until that too declined, leaving many empty ghost towns. Mining and ranching revived early in the 20th century, only to be wiped out again following the Wall Street Crash of 1929.

In the early 1930s the state government passed the legislation that legalized gambling and prostitution and made marriage licences and divorces easy to obtain. Tourism boomed, the economy grew, and more orthodox industry was boosted by cheap hydroelectricity from the Hoover Dam on the Colorado River and by the discovery of further mineral deposits.

NEW HAMPSHIRE

Nickname	Granite State
Ratified the Constitution	1788
Capital	Concord
Area	24,032 sq km (9,279 sq mi)
Population	1,314,895
Outstanding features	Mount Washington, Lake Winnipesaukee
Principal industries	machinery, electronics, plastics, tourism

New Hampshire

New Hampshire was first settled by Europeans in the 17th century. The Protestants who sailed here named their new home for the English county of Hampshire. Portsmouth, Dover, and Exeter, founded in the 1620s, were also named for their English counterparts. From 1719 a wave of Scots-Irish settlers began to arrive, founding the towns of Londonderry and Dublin.

A leader in the Revolutionary cause, the state announced its declaration of independence several weeks before the national declaration was made in 1776. Today, New Hampshire adheres strongly to its traditional democratic institutions, notably the meetings that are held every year in each town.

In recent decades the state has welcomed new industries, particularly electronics manufacture, plastics, and service industries. Tourism thrives on old-world villages, forest scenery, fall colors, and winter skiing.

NEW JERSEY

Nickname	Garden State
Ratified the Constitution	1787
Capital	Trenton
Area	20,168 sq km (7,787 sq mi)
Population	8,724,560
Outstanding features	Kittatinny Mountains, Pine Barrens (heath, dunes, and woodland)
Principal industries	chemicals, electrical machinery, scientific research

New Jersey

New Jersey harbors many contradictions. Although it is known as the Garden State it is often crowded and industrialized, plagued by pollution, and has a reputation for organized crime. Conversely, the long stretches of good beaches along the Atlantic Ocean are a major attraction for tourists.

In the forefront of the industrial revolution, north-central New Jersey became the main transportation hub of the Eastern Seaboard. The south developed into a truck-farming area, growing salads and vegetables for city markets—hence the state's nickname. After the Civil War liberal commerce laws led to runaway industrialization, only partly curbed by federal legislation in 1913. The United States relied heavily on the state's industrial capacity in both world wars.

Northeastern New Jersey is now an overspill area for neighboring New York City and is home to highways that are among the world's busiest.

NEW MEXICO

Nickname Land of Enchantment

Joined the Union 1912

Capital Santa Fe

Area 314,924 sq km (121,593 sq mi)

Population 1,954,599

Outstanding features Wheeler Peak (Rocky Mountains), Carlsbad Caverns

Principal industries mining, tourism, foodstuffs

New Mexico

In 1540 Francisco Vásquez de Coronado (1510–54) came to the area in search of the legendary "seven cities of gold," but left empty-handed. In the 17th century the first European settlements were built by Juan de Oñate (1550–1630), including Santa Fe in 1610. The colony was later destroyed by Native Americans defending their way of life. In the 18th century Spain regained control, and in 1821 the area became part of Mexico. The eastern section was annexed by the United States in 1845. During the subsequent Mexican War the whole area was occupied by the Army of the West, before Mexico finally ceded it to the United States in 1848. Conflict with the Navajo and Apache peoples are the stuff of Wild West legend, but the arrival of the railroad in 1880 brought a massive wave of immigration by white settlers.

During World War II the atomic bomb was developed at Los Alamos to the northeast of Santa Fe, and scientific research remains an important activity. Today agriculture is limited because of the low rainfall, but cattle ranching is important. The state attracts many tourists, and there is a thriving market for Native American and Mexican craft souvenirs, such as pottery, blankets, and silver jewelry. Oil and gas development also contribute to the state economy.

More than one-third of the population is of Spanish origin, about half of them Mexican Americans, and Spanish is the state's second official language. Santa Fe is the highest capital city in the United States at about 2,135 m (7,000 ft) above sea level.

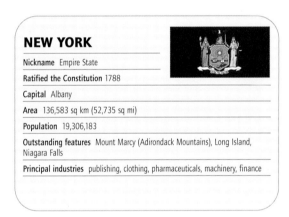

NEW YORK

Nickname Empire State

Ratified the Constitution 1788

Capital Albany

Area 136,583 sq km (52,735 sq mi)

Population 19,306,183

Outstanding features Mount Marcy (Adirondack Mountains), Long Island, Niagara Falls

Principal industries publishing, clothing, pharmaceuticals, machinery, finance

New York

The first Europeans to reach New York Bay were Giovanni da Verrazzano (c.1485–1528) in 1524 and Henry Hudson (1565–1611) in 1609. However, the original European settlers were the Dutch, who founded the colony of New Amsterdam on Manhattan Island. In 1664 the British took the colony by force, renaming it New York. As one of the 13 original colonies, New York, and New York City in particular, reflects the diversity of its immigrant settlers, originally from Italy, Germany, Russia, Poland, Ireland, and Puerto Rico.

Today's New York City is among the world's most populous cities and is a national center for finance and the arts. It is also the nation's largest seaport and has three international airports within the metropolitan area. So dominant is New York City that the rest of the state is often forgotten, but upstate New York contains a variety of landscapes, from the Great Lakes and Niagara Falls in the west via the mountains, lakes, and magnificent fall colors of the Appalachian Mountains to the Hudson Valley in the east.

On September 11, 2001, New York City was the target of a terrorist attack that destroyed the twin towers of the World Trade Center—a symbol of the financial world. Nearly 3,000 people were killed.

NORTH CAROLINA	
Nickname Tar Heel State	
Ratified the Constitution 1789	
Capital Raleigh	
Area 136,412 sq km (52,669 sq mi)	
Population 8,856,505	
Outstanding features Mount Mitchell (Blue Ridge Mountains), Cape Hatteras, Cape Lookout	
Principal industries textiles, tobacco, electronics	

North Carolina

In 1585 the first English settlement in the New World was established on Roanoke Island but it was not until 1712 that North Carolina became a colony with its own governor. During the 1830s most of the native Cherokee population were forcibly removed to the west of the Mississippi River. North Carolina seceded from the Union in 1861 but paid dearly for doing so. Although the 1868 constitution was more liberal than some, black people were effectively denied civil rights from 1900 until the 1960s.

Today, agriculture has been largely replaced by manufacturing as the state's main source of income, but North Carolina still remains the center of the U.S. tobacco industry.

Geographical features in the west of the state are the Appalachian Mountains (including the Blue Ridge and the Great Smoky Mountains). In the east, on the string of islands called the Outer Banks, coastal erosion has led to the resiting of at least one well-known landmark—the Cape Hatteras lighthouse. Wilbur and Orville Wright (1867–1912 and 1871–1948) made the first successful powered manned flight, in 1903, near Kitty Hawk.

The Little Missouri River winding through Wind Canyon in the Theodore Roosevelt National Park, North Dakota.

NORTH DAKOTA	
Nickname Flickertail State	
Joined the Union 1889	
Capital Bismarck	
Area 183,117 sq km (70,702 sq mi)	
Population 635,867	
Outstanding features North Dakota Badlands, Missouri River, Lake Sakakawea	
Principal industries foodstuffs, petroleum extraction, agricultural machinery	

North Dakota

North Dakota is a leading agricultural state, the cool subhumid climate of its northerly location being ideal for growing wheat and for cattle ranching. Although agriculture still dominates, the state is also a leading producer of petroleum and hydroelectricity.

The area was acquired by the United States from the French, partly in the Louisiana Purchase of 1803 and partly as the result of a treaty with Britain in 1813. The earliest settlers, in Pembina in 1812, were of Irish and Scottish descent. They were followed at the end of the century by Germans and Norwegians.

Native Americans were exploited and became vulnerable to "white man's" diseases such as smallpox. Gold prospectors, who traveled northwest along the Missouri River, encroached onto Native American land and caused further serious conflict.

The arrival of the railroads in 1861 brought a massive wave of settlement and an agricultural boom. In 1889 the Dakota Territory was divided, and both North and South Dakota joined the Union. Farming remains the dominant interest, protected at first by political means and later by a cooperative movement.

OHIO

Nickname	Buckeye State
Joined the Union	1803
Capital	Columbus
Area	115,998 sq km (44,787 sq mi)
Population	11,478,006
Outstanding features	Sandusky Bay (Lake Erie), Miami River
Principal industries	transportation equipment, machinery

Ohio

With Pennsylvania to the east and Indiana to the west, Ohio forms a bridge between the original states of the Union and the Midwest. It was the Union's 17th state.

In prehistoric times Ohio was the home of the Hopewell peoples. Excavation of their large burial mounds and earthworks has revealed a highly sophisticated culture that made finely crafted artifacts.

In the 18th century possession of the area was contested by Britain and France. Eventual statehood was followed by swift settlement, notably by Scots-Irish and German-speaking immigrants. Subsequent river, canal, and railroad links made it readily accessible from the east and, although originally agricultural, the state quickly became industrialized, especially after the civil

Wheat fields in the rich, rolling landscape of Ohio. The state combines agriculture with a strong manufacturing industry.

War. This led to the growth of cities such as Cleveland on the shores of Lake Erie and Cincinnati on the Ohio River. Today the state combines a rich agricultural landscape with an extensive manufacturing base. Traditional industries such as coal mining are in decline but have been replaced by other heavy industries, for example, the manufacture of electrical machinery.

The town of Dayton was the home of pioneer aviators Wilbur and Orville Wright (1867–1912 and 1871–1948)—hence the state's long association with the aviation industry.

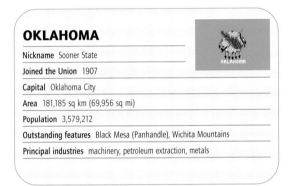

OKLAHOMA

Nickname	Sooner State
Joined the Union	1907
Capital	Oklahoma City
Area	181,185 sq km (69,956 sq mi)
Population	3,579,212
Outstanding features	Black Mesa (Panhandle), Wichita Mountains
Principal industries	machinery, petroleum extraction, metals

Oklahoma

The area was acquired by the United States from France as part of the 1803 Louisiana Purchase. In 1828 Congress created an Indian Territory that was reserved exclusively for Native Americans. It consisted of five republics or nations, subsequently known as Oklahoma,

from the Choctaw words meaning "red people." In the Civil War the Native Americans, unhappy with the federal government, sided with the Confederate army and suffered accordingly. In 1889 Congress allowed homesteaders to open up the Indian Territory land for farming, and Oklahoma was swamped by a series of "land runs." Today only a minority of the population is Native American.

A mining boom brought other settlers, but farming remained the most important occupation of the new state. However, many farmers lost their land and their livelihood during the dustbowl years of the 1930s, although new prosperity arrived with the discovery of massive petroleum reserves in the state.

OREGON

Nickname Sunset State	
Joined the Union 1859	
Capital Salem	
Area 251,418 sq km (97,073 sq mi)	
Population 3,700,758	
Outstanding features Mount Hood (Cascade Range), Crater Lake National Park, Columbia River Gorge	
Principal industries timber products, machinery, foodstuffs	

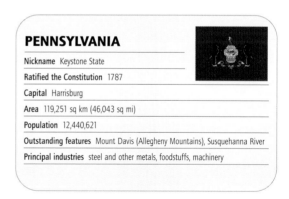

STATE OF OREGON · 1859

Oregon

First claimed by both Britain and Spain in the 16th century, the area—and its Native American population—

remained largely undisturbed until 1792, when Robert Cray (1755-1806) entered from the west via the Columbia River. Fur traders arrived from the east, having followed the 3,200-km (2,000-mi) Oregon Trail which ran from Independence, Missouri, and set up the Pacific Fur Company. Subsequent decades saw a growing tide of settlement, much of it in the Williamette Valley between the Cascade and Coast Mountain ranges. In 1842 Britain abandoned its claim to Oregon. The state still depends largely on farmland and forestry for its prosperity, but the economy has become more diversified in recent decades. Tourism plays an increasingly important part, largely because of the spectacular coastline, with its famous sand dunes, and the magnificent mountain scenery.

Oregon was among the first states to introduce stringent control of vehicle-exhaust emissions. The eco-friendly city of Portland has an extensive and easy-to-use public transportation system, to the extent that many of its residents have ignored the national trend and have abandoned their automobiles.

PENNSYLVANIA

Nickname Keystone State	
Ratified the Constitution 1787	
Capital Harrisburg	
Area 119,251 sq km (46,043 sq mi)	
Population 12,440,621	
Outstanding features Mount Davis (Allegheny Mountains), Susquehanna River	
Principal industries steel and other metals, foodstuffs, machinery	

Pennsylvania

One of the oldest and most populous states, Pennsylvania extends westward from the Delaware River to the shores of Lake Erie. Its official name, the Commonwealth of Pennsylvania, reflects the idealism of its founder, William Penn (1644–1718) who, in 1681, was granted land by Charles II of England (1630–85). The following year Penn founded his colony on the site of present-day Philadelphia and based it on the Quaker principles of tolerance and democracy. He was notably honest in his dealings with Native Americans, and

Quaker policies encouraged many minorities—the Pennsylvania Dutch, the Mennonites, and the Amish—to settle in the colony. One of the original 13 states, it was the site of a major Civil War battle, which saw a Union victory at Gettysburg in 1863.

Pennsylvania's fortunes were originally founded on its rich agricultural land. Huge mineral deposits subsequently helped make it America's first industrial and manufacturing center, especially around Pittsburgh, where "steel kings" such as Andrew Carnegie (1835-1919) established enormous plants. Traditional industries have since declined, but Pennsylvania remains a primarily industrial state, although much of the land is still cultivated for agricultural purposes.

The city of Philadelphia is a world-famous cultural center, with its art collections, orchestras, and museums. Pittsburgh, transformed by a dramatic clean-up campaign, is rapidly achieving the same status.

RHODE ISLAND

Nickname	Little Rhody
Ratified the Constitution	1790
Capital	Providence
Area	3,139 sq km (1,212 sq mi)
Population	1,067,610
Outstanding feature	Narragansett Bay
Principal industries	jewelry, machinery, textiles, electronics

Rhode Island

The smallest state in the Union, located on New England's Atlantic seaboard, Rhode Island takes its name from one of several islands situated in Narragansett Bay. The first European settlement was Providence, founded in 1836 by the Puritan minister Roger Williams (1603-83), after his exile from Massachusetts as the result of his religious dissent. A strict disciplinarian, Williams managed nevertheless to maintain a spirit of religious tolerance. He also dealt honestly with the local Native Americans.

The state's independent tradition made the colony swift to rebel but slow to join the new nation. It was the last of the original 13 colonies to ratify the

Constitution, and the last to introduce adult universal suffrage—the subject of Dorr's Rebellion in 1842.

Economically, Rhode Island was at the forefront in the industrial revolution. Today its economy relies on sophisticated light industries—such as electronics—and on the service sector. Although it is the second most densely populated state, Rhode Island retains strong historical roots, particularly in the old seaports of Providence and Newport, where whole districts are carefully preserved and include some of the oldest buildings in the United States. Every summer the state hosts the world-famous Newport Jazz Festival.

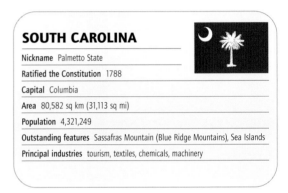

SOUTH CAROLINA

Nickname	Palmetto State
Ratified the Constitution	1788
Capital	Columbia
Area	80,582 sq km (31,113 sq mi)
Population	4,321,249
Outstanding features	Sassafras Mountain (Blue Ridge Mountains), Sea Islands
Principal industries	tourism, textiles, chemicals, machinery

South Carolina

In 1670 British colonists built a settlement at Albemarle Point. Living conditions later drove them to Charles Town—named after Charles II of England (1630-85)—near the mouth of the Ashley River. Ten years later the town was rebuilt, as Charleston, on the other side of the river, and grew wealthy from its trade in rice, pelts, and indigo. Crown control of the colony's finances caused resentment and led to South Carolina's support for the American Revolution.

Cotton plantations brought wealth to the state, but dependence on slavery led to secession from the Union in 1861. An engagement with Federal troops at Fort Sumter in Charleston Harbor subsequently triggered the Civil War. In 1865, at the end of the war, Union troops caused widespread destruction, which included the burning of Columbia. The state was readmitted to the Union in 1868, but racial tensions continued and were reflected in the 1895 Constitution. Black civil rights were not restored until the 1960s.

In the late 1800s tenant farming (sharecropping) saw tobacco and soybeans replace rice and cotton as the main crops. After 1900 textiles became the state's main industry. Today South Carolina's economy is industrial rather than agricultural. Tourism is also thriving, thanks to the old-world atmosphere and the warm climate of its coastal towns.

SOUTH DAKOTA	
Nickname Coyote State	
Joined the Union 1889	
Capital Pierre	
Area 199,730 sq km (77,136 sq mi)	
Population 781,919	
Outstanding features Mount Rushmore (Black Hills), Badlands National Park	
Principal industries foodstuffs, machinery, electronics	

South Dakota

Acquired by the United States from France as part of the 1803 Louisiana Purchase, South Dakota was separated from North Dakota in 1889. Fifteen years previously gold had been found in the Black Hills, an area previously forbidden to Europeans by a treaty with the Teton Dakota peoples. But the Native Americans were soon routed in battle and, in 1877, were forced to cede the area. Freight and stage lines into nearby Rapid City soon brought a steady flow of prospectors and settlers from the east. Between 1878 and 1887 the population quadrupled.

The region offered pastureland as well as gold, and in the early 1900s cattlemen took further parcels of Native American land. Since then drought and depression—notably the dustbowl years of the 1930s—have taken their toll. Farming remains the chief source of income, but manufacturing and tourism are also contributing to the economy.

Mount Rushmore, in the Black Hills, is home to the giant carvings of the heads of presidents Washington, Jefferson, Lincoln, and Theodore Roosevelt. The state is also known for its "Wild West" past. This includes the town of Deadwood and its cemetery, where Calamity Jane and Wild Bill Hickok are buried.

The stunning Great Smoky Mountains of Tennessee are a major range in the southern part of the Appalachian Mountains.

TENNESSEE	
Nickname Volunteer State	
Joined the Union 1796	
Capital Nashville	
Area 109,152 sq km (42,144 sq mi)	
Population 6,038,803	
Outstanding features Clingmans Dome (Smoky Mountains), Great Appalachian Valley	
Principal industries chemicals, foodstuffs, machinery	

Tennessee

The region, acquired by Britain in 1763 after a seven-year conflict with France, was occupied by settlers from Virginia and the Carolinas. In 1789 it separated from North Carolina and became a state seven years later. Before the Civil War there was loyalty to the Union, but divisions appeared. Tennessee became a key battleground, second only to Virginia. After the war, in 1865, the white supremacist Ku Klux Klan was born at Pulaski (south of Nashville). Black people were effectively segregated from the 1870s until the 1960s.

From the 1940s power from the Tennessee Valley hydroelectric scheme fueled industrial development, ending the state's reliance on agriculture. There is now a move toward the trade and services sector, and tourism has become important. Many come to visit Nashville, the heart of Country and Western music.

TEXAS

Nickname	Lone Star State
Joined the Union	1845
Capital	Austin
Area	691,027 sq km (266,807 sq mi)
Population	23,507,783
Outstanding features	Mount Livermore, Guadalupe Peak, Big Bend National Park
Principal industries	petroleum, machinery, foodstuffs, clothing

Texas

Until Alaska was admitted to the Union in 1959, Texas was the largest state. Its alluvial plains extend inland from the Gulf of Mexico, rising to meet the Great Plains to the north. The southwestern border with Mexico is formed by the waters of the Rio Grande. The first Spanish explorers found the area sparsely inhabited by Native American peoples. The region remained under Spanish rule until a coup in Mexico in 1833 drove the Anglo-American settlers to stage a rebellion with the aim of declaring independence. In 1836, following the famous siege of the Alamo, the Texans routed the Mexicans at San Jacinto. Texas joined the Union nine years later.

The state seceded from the Union in 1861 and came under martial law during Reconstruction. In the 1870s and 1880s Native Americans were expelled, railroad construction opened up, and a boom in cattle ranching created the archetypal "Wild West" state.

In 1901 petroleum was discovered, leading to an even greater boom, and Houston and Dallas became two of the most affluent cities in the world. A range of industries followed, although agriculture has retained its importance, especially in the areas of cotton and livestock production. Recent years have seen a growth in the electronics and consumer product sectors.

UTAH

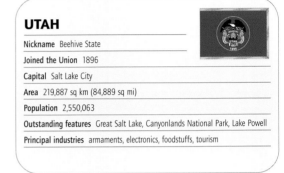

Nickname	Beehive State
Joined the Union	1896
Capital	Salt Lake City
Area	219,887 sq km (84,889 sq mi)
Population	2,550,063
Outstanding features	Great Salt Lake, Canyonlands National Park, Lake Powell
Principal industries	armaments, electronics, foodstuffs, tourism

Utah

The landscape of Utah is generally barren, arid, and spectacular. It has nurtured some hardy peoples and some distinctive cultures. Among them, in about 400 A.D., were the Anasazi, or Pueblo, peoples. Their society disappeared before the arrival of the Spanish in the 18th century, but their cliff villages survive, along with pottery and rock paintings. Their place was taken by the Navajo and Ute peoples.

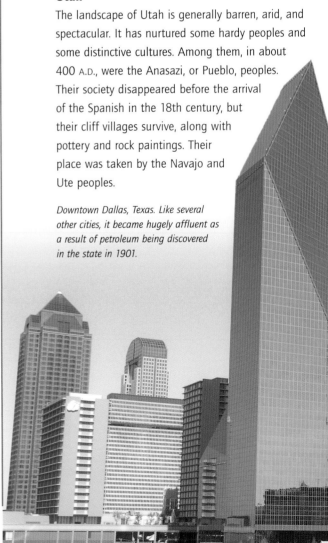

Downtown Dallas, Texas. Like several other cities, it became hugely affluent as a result of petroleum being discovered in the state in 1901.

In 1848 the area was annexed from Mexico. At the same time, members of the Church of Jesus Christ of Latter-day Saints—or Mormons—led by Brigham Young (1801-77) fled persecution as a result of their belief in polygamy, and settled in the Great Salt Lake Valley. Following clashes over food supplies, Native Americans were removed to reservations, but by the 1890s the Mormons had established a stable community based largely on agriculture. A disapproving Congress refused statehood applications until polygamy was renounced in 1896. Today, Mormon influence endures, Salt Lake City has become a major financial and commercial center, and Utah is a popular tourist destination.

VERMONT

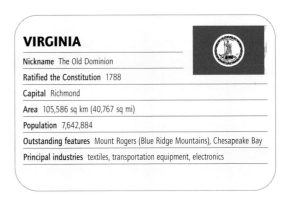

Nickname Green Mountain State

Joined the Union 1791

Capital Montpelier

Area 24,900 sq km (9,614 sq mi)

Population 623,908

Outstanding features Mount Mansfield, Lake Champlain

Principal industries tourism, furniture, machine tools, microelectronics

Vermont

One of the most historic states, Vermont is also one of the most beautiful, its glorious fall colors being justly famous. The French were the first to establish outposts in the area, which was a hunting ground of the Native American peoples, but in the 18th century the Dutch and the British became permanent settlers.

The Green Mountain Boys, a band of armed irregulars organized to protect Vermont from New York's territorial claims, supported the Revolution but also resisted the Union. In 1777 they declared Vermont an independent republic. It remained so until 1791. An influx of settlers cleared extensive areas of forest, but the land was stony, and cultivation was difficult. By the 1830s most settlers had moved westward. During the Civil War, Vermont saw the only action north of Pennsylvania—a Canada-based Confederate raid.

Industries are light and include computers and precision engineering. A favorite holiday area, Vermont provides tranquillity in summer and skiing in winter. Artistic and literary communities flourish, along with famous colleges such as Bennington and Marlboro.

VIRGINIA

Nickname The Old Dominion

Ratified the Constitution 1788

Capital Richmond

Area 105,586 sq km (40,767 sq mi)

Population 7,642,884

Outstanding features Mount Rogers (Blue Ridge Mountains), Chesapeake Bay

Principal industries textiles, transportation equipment, electronics

Virginia

Britain's first colony, established in 1607, was chafing at British rule long before the War of Independence, with notable Virginians George Washington (1732-99) and Thomas Jefferson (1743-1826) playing a leading part. Importing slaves was abolished in 1778, although slavery itself was maintained. In 1861 Virginia led the Confederacy, whose capital was at Richmond. Virginia's economy suffered until long after the Civil War. By World War I, manufacturing had superseded agriculture, and World War II brought prosperity with shipbuilding and military bases. Virginia's proudest possession is its history, with sites such as Williamsburg and Mount Vernon attracting a thriving tourist trade.

Mount Rainier National Park, Washington. Mount Rainier itself is the state's highest point, at 4,392 m (14,40 ft) above sea level.

WASHINGTON

Nickname	Evergreen State
Joined the Union	1889
Capital	Olympia
Area	176,479 sq km (68,139 sq mi)
Population	6,395,798
Outstanding features	Mount Rainier (Cascade Range), Puget Sound
Principal industries	aircraft, wood and paper products, foodstuffs, information technology

Washington

During the 16th century European navigators, searching for a Northwest Passage to Asia, discovered the existence of the Pacific Northwest. The area that is now Washington State was once part of the Oregon Country, whose northern boundary was set in 1846 along the present Canadian frontier. White settlers moved into the area along the Oregon Trail. In 1853 Washington became a separate territory.

Railroad construction in the 1880s brought growth, and Washington became a base for gold prospectors and miners heading for Alaska and the Klondike. The 20th century saw the damming of the Columbia River to provide power, irrigation, and improved navigation. Traditionally, the economy has been largely dependent on natural resources such as forestry. In recent years Seattle has become a major economic center and is home to software companies such as Microsoft. The state is also a center for the aerospace industry.

In 1980 ash from the volcanic eruption of Mount St. Helens caused massive environmental damage and temporarily disrupted the tourist economy.

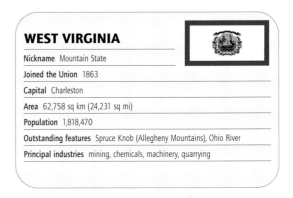

WEST VIRGINIA

Nickname	Mountain State
Joined the Union	1863
Capital	Charleston
Area	62,758 sq km (24,231 sq mi)
Population	1,818,470
Outstanding features	Spruce Knob (Allegheny Mountains), Ohio River
Principal industries	mining, chemicals, machinery, quarrying

West Virginia

This Appalachian state, carved by swift rivers and covered by dense forest, was once home to various Native American peoples, notably the Hopewell, whose prehistoric earthworks can be found near Charleston. Although Virginia belongs firmly to the South, West Virginia has always had more in common with the northern states. Virginia seceded from the Union in 1861, but the people in the northwest refused to follow them into the Confederacy; thus the state of West Virginia was born.

After the Civil War the expansion of the railroad network brought industrial development to the mountains, where local resources included limestone, salt, and coal. Agriculture and mining have declined, but petroleum and natural gas have been added to the list of resources. Tourism is also expanding.

WISCONSIN

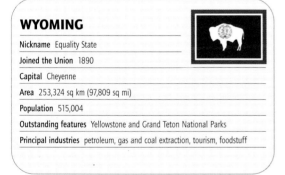

Nickname	Badger State
Joined the Union	1848
Capital	Madison
Area	171,496 sq km (66,215 sq mi)
Population	5,556,506
Outstanding features	Lake Winnebago, Door Peninsula (Lake Michigan), Apostle Islands (Lake Superior)
Principal industries	foodstuffs, machinery, metals, wood and paper processing

Wisconsin

Once an area of wild forests inhabited by Native American peoples such as the Winnebago, Wisconsin has become a more urban and industrialized state. The area came under British control in 1763, was ceded to the United States in 1783, became part of Northwest Territory in 1787, and formed part of Indiana Territory in 1800. European immigrants arrived in the 19th century. The Black Hawk War of 1832 shattered Native American power, and in 1836 Wisconsin Territory was created. Statehood followed 12 years later.

Today Wisconsin is a leading supplier of dairy products. Manufacturing and processing are equally important, and tourism plays a significant role.

WYOMING

Nickname	Equality State
Joined the Union	1890
Capital	Cheyenne
Area	253,324 sq km (97,809 sq mi)
Population	515,004
Outstanding features	Yellowstone and Grand Teton National Parks
Principal industries	petroleum, gas and coal extraction, tourism, foodstuff

Wyoming

When the United States bought this area from France as part of the 1803 Louisiana Purchase, it was still a mountainous wilderness inhabited by the Arapaho and Shoshoni peoples. For many years the arid prairies and mountains discouraged settlement, and the area was little more than a staging point for people heading westward along the Oregon and Overland Trails. The arrival of the telegraph and railroad led to retaliatory raids by the Arapaho and Shoshoni, whose lands were taken and hunting grounds disturbed. By 1869, however, most of the Native Americans had been confined to the Wind River Reservation on the eastern slopes of the Rockies.

Cattle ranchers followed the railroads, and large areas of the state remain as pastureland. However, mineral fuel production is now the dominant industry, and uranium and hydroelectricity have made the region a leading producer of power. Wyoming was the first state to create national parks such as Yellowstone (including the geyser Old Faithful) and Grand Teton, with the result that tourism has benefited accordingly. It was also the first state to give women the vote—hence its nickname of the Equality State.

DISTRICT OF COLUMBIA

Federal territory authorized	1790
Coterminous with the United States capital	Washington, DC
Area	179 sq km (69 sq mi)
Population	581,530
Outstanding feature	Potomac River
Principal industries	federal administration, tourism

District of Columbia

The District of Columbia (Washington, DC)—often simply referred to as "DC" to avoid any confusion with Washington State—is the seat of the federal government. Lying on the northern banks of the Potomac River, between Maryland and Virginia, its buildings include the White House, the Pentagon, and the Capitol—where the Senate and the House of Representatives meet. It is also home to the Library of Congress, the National Archives, the Smithsonian Institution, and important museums. Its impressive embassies and government officials' homes, however, almost rub shoulders with the slums that saw serious race riots in the 1960s. Some of these poor areas have subsequently been cleared in urban renewal programs.

MEXICO

Mexico, a large expanse of mountainous land lying between the Pacific Ocean and the Gulf of Mexico, is one of the largest of the Latin American states. It possesses a colorful diversity of cultures and racial mixes, which owe much to its complex and frequently violent history. However, the country's rich natural resources and swift economic growth have been largely offset by the rapid rise in the population. A large foreign debt, high inflation, unemployment, falling oil prices, and earthquakes have also taken their toll.

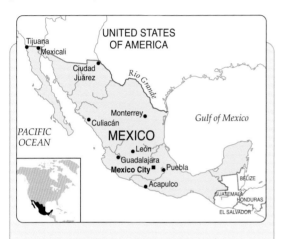

NATIONAL DATA - MEXICO

Land area	1,923,040 sq km (742,490 sq mi)			

Climate		Temperatures		Annual
	Altitude m (ft)	January °C(°F)	July °C(°F)	precipitation mm (in)
Mexico City	2,306 (7,564)	14 (56)	17 (63	816 (32.1)

Major physical features highest point: Ciltlaltépetl 5,610 m (18,406 ft); longest river: Rio Grande (part) 3,060 km (1,900 mi)

Population (2006 est.) 107,449,525

Form of government federal multiparty republic with two legislative houses

Armed forces army 144,000; navy 37,000; air force 11,770

Largest cities Mexico City (capital – 8,658,576); Ecatepec* (1,884,585); Guadalajara (1,632,171); Ciudad Juarez (1,496,551); Tijuana (1,482,294); Puebla (1,441,685); Nezahualcóyotl (1,229,673); León (1,156,053); Monterrey (1,123,799); Zapopan† (1,022,564) * part of Mexico City Metropolitan area † part of Guadalajara Metropolitan area

Official language Spanish

Ethnic composition Mestizo (Amerindian-Spanish) 60%; Amerindian or predominantly Amerindian 30%; White 9%; other 1%

Religious affiliations Roman Catholic 89%; Protestant 6%; other 5%

Currency 1 New Mexican peso (MXN) = 100 centavos

Gross domestic product (2006 est.) U.S. $1.134 trillion

Gross domestic product per capita (2006 est.) U.S. $10,600

Life expectancy at birth male 72.63 yr; female 78.33 yr

Major resources petroleum, silver, copper, gold, lead, zinc, natural gas, hydropower, timber; textiles; iron and steel; petrochemicals; beverages, fisheries, tourism, coffee, cotton, fruit and vegetables, aluminium, sorghum, sugarcane

Geography

Many parts of Mexico are subject to earthquakes and volcanic eruptions. The broad, tapering arc of the country is framed by the lowlying Yucatán Peninsula extending northward from the Belize border and the long, mountainous peninsula of Baja California that runs parallel to the west coast. The area between Mexico's Gulf and Pacific coastlines is occupied by a massive central plateau rising in the south to the Mesa Central. It is crossed by volcanoes such as Popacatépetl and bounded by the mountains of the Sierra Madre.

Climate varies with altitude and latitude. Desert predominates in the north, but rainfall increases in the southeast, the heaviest falls being along the Gulf coast and in the south. The coastal plains and foothills of the Sierra Madre can experience violent hurricanes. High in

The ancient city of Teotihuacán. This culture extended its influence over central Mexico between the 2nd and 6th centuries A.D.

largely destroyed by Spanish invaders in the 16th century—the Spanish ruled harshly until independence in 1821. Mexico later became a republic. In 1845 it tried to resist the annexation of Texas by the United States, and a bitter war followed. Civil war broke out in the 1850s, and in 1910 revolutionary groups began a long struggle, resulting in the creation of a single National Revolutionary Party in 1929. For several decades it remained the dominant political force, but its narrow victory at the polls in 2006 led to a lengthy dispute and mass protests over election fraud.

Economy

Mexico has little good agricultural land—mostly on the central plateau—and much food is imported. Export crops include coffee, sugarcane, and cotton, while staples include corn, squash, and kidney beans. Cattle are reared mainly in the north. Fishing is largely for export and includes tuna, sardines, and shrimp.

Forests yield timber and chicle (for chewing gum) but are under threat by clearance. Mexico is the world's leading supplier of silver; other minerals include copper, zinc, and lead. Hydrocarbon reserves bring in the majority of foreign exchange earnings. Petrochemicals and hydroelectricity provide power. Manufacturing industries, mainly based around Mexico City, include chemicals, automobiles, iron and steel, food processing, and textiles. Trade with the United States dominates Mexico's international commerce.

the Mesa Central temperatures are low. Vegetation includes desert scrub in the north, grassland in central regions, tropical and temperate rain forest in the east, and deciduous woodland along the Pacific coastline. Animal life is diverse and includes jaguars, monkeys, parrots, anteaters, armadillos, pumas, and coyotes.

Society

Mexico's long history includes sophisticated indigenous civilizations such as the Olmecs, the Maya, and the Aztecs, which left a rich and varied cultural heritage in the form of buildings, jewelry, carvings, and hieroglyphic manuscripts. The Aztec empire was

THE PEOPLE OF MEXICO

About one-third of the population is Amerindian, while over half is mestizo (mixed race). The official language is Spanish, but some 50 Amerindian languages are spoken. More than two-thirds of Mexicans live in around the three largest cities, but emigration to the United States (often illegal) has caused friction. Subsidized healthcare is available to many, but facilities in rural areas are poor, and diseases such as malaria are common. Adequate housing is also a problem, especially in cities. There are minimum-wage laws, but rural poverty is widespread. Literacy levels are high, but rural areas lack facilities.

Mountain ranges, forests, and plains dominate the landscape of Guatemala. The climate is mostly tropical. Wildlife includes jaguars, peccaries, monkeys, crocodiles, and manatees. Once the heart of the Maya civilization, the country later experienced Spanish rule and then dictator-presidents. The economy is based on coffee exports. Cattle are raised on Pacific coast pastures. There are small mineral reserves, but industry is mainly confined to the processing of agricultural products.

Belize's landscape ranges from a swampy plain in the north to a mountainous plateau in the south. Coral islands form a chain along the coast. Forests and savanna harbor wildlife including pumas and crocodiles. The climate is subtropical, and hurricanes are common. The Maya once dominated the area. In 1862 it became British Honduras, becoming independent as Belize in 1981. Agriculture is the mainstay of the economy, with sugarcane the main crop. Manufacturing is small scale.

NATIONAL DATA – GUATEMALA

Land area 108,430 sq km (41,865 sq mi)

Climate	Altitude m (ft)	Temperatures January °C(°F)	July °C(°F)	Annual precipitation mm (in)
Guatemala	1,480 (4,856)	18 (64)	20 (68)	1,186 (46.7)

Major physical features highest point: Tajumulco ken 4,220 m (13,845 ft)

Population (2006 est.) 12,293,545

Form of government multiparty republic with one legislative house

Armed forces army 27,000; navy 1,500; air force 700

Largest cities Guatemala City (capital – 1,024,101); Mixco* (540,348); Villa Nueva* (499,133); Quezaltenango (140,405)
*Port of Guatemala City Metropolitan area

Official language Spanish

Ethnic composition Mestizo (Ladino) and European 59.4%; K'iche 9.1%; Kaqchikel 8.4%; Mam 7.9%; Q'eqchi 6.3%; other Mayan 8.6%; indigenous non-Mayan 0.2%; other 0.1%

Religious affiliations Roman Catholic 75%; Protestant 25%

Currency 1 quetzal (Q) = 100 centavos

Gross domestic product (2006 est.) U.S. $60.57 billion

Gross domestic product per capita (2006 est.) U.S. $4,900

Life expectancy at birth male 67.65 yr; female 71.18 yr

Major resources petroleum, nickel, fisheries, chicle, hydropower, bananas, cardamom, cattle, coffee, cotton, lead, maize/corn, rice, sugar beet, timber, tobacco

NATIONAL DATA – BELIZE

Land area 22,806 sq km (8,805 sq mi)

Climate	Altitude m (ft)	Temperatures January °C(°F)	July °C(°F)	Annual precipitation mm (in)
Belmopan	41 (135)	23 (73)	27 (81)	1,890 (74.4)

Major physical features highest point: Victoria Peak 1,122 m (3,681 ft)

Population (2006 est.) 287,730

Form of government multiparty constitutional monarchy with two legislative houses

Armed forces army 1,050

Largest cities Belize City (66,140); San Ignacio (18,334); Belmopan (capital – 15,940); Orange Walk (15,927); Dangriga (11,512)

Official language English

Ethnic composition Mestizo 48.7%; Creole 24.9%; Maya 10.6%; Garifuna 6.1%; other 9.7%

Religious affiliations Roman Catholic 49.6%; Protestant 27% (Pentecostal 7.4%; Anglican 5.3%; Seventh-Day Adventist 5.2%; Mennonite 4.1%; Methodist 3.5%; Jehovah's Witnesses 1.5%); other 14%; none 9.4%

Currency 1 Belize dollar (BZD) = 100 cents

Gross domestic product (2006 est.) U.S. $2.307 billion

Gross domestic product per capita (2006 est.) U.S. $8,400

Life expectancy at birth male 66.43 yr; female 70.26 yr

Major resources sugarcane,, tourism, timber, fisheries, hydropower, bananas, citrus fruits, coconuts, fish, maize/corn, rice

EL SALVADOR

The smallest and most densely populated country in Central America, El Salvador's landscape is a mixture of plains, mountains, and river valleys. The country is prone to earthquakes. Grasslands and forest grow, but much of the land is cultivated. Spanish invaders overran the indigenous peoples in the 1500s, and in recent times dictatorships, guerrilla wars, and civil wars have punctuated politics. Coffee is the main export crop, along with sugarcane, corn, and cotton. A white elite owned most farms, but many have been redistributed. Investment in the 1970s initiated many new industries, but civil war damaged the infrastructure and economy.

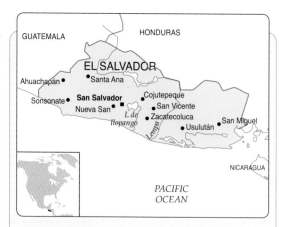

NATIONAL DATA - EL SALVADOR

Land area 20,720 sq km (8,000 sq mi)

Climate	Altitude m (ft)	Temperatures January °C(°F)	July °C(°F)	Annual precipitation mm (in)
San Salvador	682 (2,238)	23 (73)	25 (76)	1,734 (68.2)

Major physical features highest point: Izalco 2,386 m (7,828 ft); longest river: Lempa 320 km (200 mi)

Population (2006 est.) 6,822,378

Form of government multiparty republic with one legislative house

Armed forces army 13,850; navy 700; air force 950

Largest cities San Salvador (capital - 542,799); Soyapango* (340,110); Mejicanos* (164,407)   * suburbs of San Salvador

Official language Spanish

Ethnic composition Mestizo 90%; White 9%; Amerindian 1%

Religious affiliations Roman Catholic 83%; other 17%

Currency 1 United States Dollar (USD) = 100 centavos

Gross domestic product (2006 est.) U.S. $33.2 billion

Gross domestic product per capita (2006 est.) U.S. $4,900

Life expectancy at birth male 67.88 yr; female 75.28 yr

Major resources hydropower, geothermal power, petroleum, coffee, cotton, maize/corn, sugarcane, beans, cattle, poultry, rice, silver, sorghum, timber

HONDURAS

Mountainous Honduras is bisected by river valleys and bordered by coastal plains. The climate is hot and humid, although moderated by altitude inland. Coastal mangroves, savanna, and dense rain forest characterize the vegetation. Insects, birds, reptiles, jaguars, and tapirs are among the many animals. Once part of the Maya civilization, Honduras was settled by Europeans in 1522. Dictatorships and coups have punctuated recent politics. Bananas and coffee are the main export crops, but a hurricane in 1998 damaged the economy. Mineral resources have not been fully exploited.

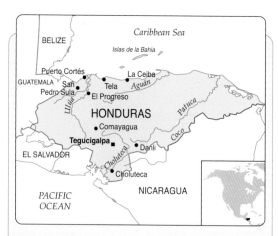

NATIONAL DATA - HONDURAS

Land area 111,890 sq km (43,201 sq mi)

Climate	Altitude m (ft)	Temperatures January °C(°F)	July °C(°F)	Annual precipitation mm (in)
Tegucigalpa	1,004 (3,294)	20 (68)	23 (73)	917 (36.1)

Major physical features highest point: Cerro Las Minas 2,827 m (9,275 ft); longest river: Coco (part) 685 km (425 mi)

Population (2006 est.) 7,326,496

Form of government multiparty republic with one legislative house

Armed forces army 8,300; navy 1,400; air force 2,300

Largest cities Tegucigalpa (joint capital with Comayaguela - 893,589); San Pedro Sula (516,608); Comayagua (61,576)

Official language Spanish

Ethnic composition Mestizo 90%; Amerindian 7%; Black 2%; White 1%

Religious affiliations Roman Catholic 97%; Protestant 3%

Currency 1 Honduran lempira (HNL) = 100 centavos

Gross domestic product (2006 est.) U.S. $22.13 billion

Gross domestic product per capita (2006 est.) U.S. $3,000

Life expectancy at birth male 67.75 yr; female 70.98 yr

Major resources timber, gold, silver, copper, lead, zinc, iron ore, antimony, coal, fisheries, hydropower, bananas, beans, cattle, coffee, fruits, maize/corn, rice, shellfish, sugarcane, timber, tin, tobacco

NICARAGUA

Nicaragua's landscape is characterized by swamps and lagoons on its Caribbean, or Mosquito, Coast. Inland there are mountains and volcanoes, and large Lake Nicaragua lies in the southeast. Severe earthquakes are common. Most of the west of the country is savanna, and the eastern half has tropical rain forest. Nicaragua was conquered by Spain in the 16th century, but gained independence in 1838. Political stability has been difficult to achieve. The chief crops are cotton, coffee, and bananas, but the economy still suffers from the effects of civil war and hurricane damage. Industrial development is limited.

NATIONAL DATA – NICARAGUA

Land area 120,254 sq km (46,430 sq mi)

Climate	Altitude m (ft)	Temperatures January °C(°F)	July °C(°F)	Annual precipitation mm (in)
Managua	55 (180)	26 (79)	27 (81)	1,141 (44.9)

Major physical features highest point: Cerro Mogotón 2,103 m (6,900 ft)

Population (2006 est.) 5,570,129

Form of government multiparty republic with one legislative house

Armed forces army 12,000; navy 800; air force 1,200

Capital city Managua (1,007,811)

Official language Spanish

Ethnic composition Mestizo 69%; White 17%; Black 9%; Amerindian 5%

Religious affiliations Roman Catholic 58.5%; Evangelical 21.5%; Moravian 1.5%; Jehovah's Witnesses 0.9%; other 1.6%; none 16%

Currency 1 córdoba (C) = 100 centavos

Gross domestic product (2006 est.) U.S. $16.83 billion

Gross domestic product per capita (2006 est.) U.S. $3,000

Life expectancy at birth male 68.55 yr; female 72.81 yr

Major resources gold, silver, copper, tungsten, lead, zinc, timber, fisheries, bananas, cattle, coffee, cotton, maize/corn, rice, sugarcane

COSTA RICA

Costa Rica's narrow Pacific and Caribbean coasts have mangroves and white sandy beaches. Inland the terrain is mountainous, and in places volcanic eruptions and earthquakes are rife. Thick forest grows in the coastal lowlands, and a huge variety of animal life abounds. Unusually for Central America, Nicaragua is populated mainly by people of European descent. Earthquakes, falling coffee prices, foreign debt, and an influx of refugees have all damaged the economy, which is based on coffee and bananas. Manufactures for export include medicines, metals, and machinery.

NATIONAL DATA – COSTA RICA

Land area 50,660 sq km (19,600 sq mi)

Climate	Altitude m (ft)	Temperatures January °C(°F)	July °C(°F)	Annual precipitation mm (in)
San José	1,146 (3,760)	19 (67)	21 (69)	1,866 (73.4)

Major physical features highest point: Mount Chirripó 3,820 m (12,533 ft)

Population (2006 est.) 4,075,261

Form of government multiparty republic with one legislative house

Armed forces paramilitary 8,400

Capital city San José (342,977)

Official language Spanish

Ethnic composition White (including Mestizo) 94%; Black 3%; Amerindian 1%; Chinese 1%; other 1%

Religious affiliations Roman Catholic 76.3%; Evangelical 13.7%; Jehovah's Witnesses 1.3%; other Protestant 0.7%; other 4.8%; none 3.2%

Currency 1 Costa Rican colón (CRC) = 100 céntimos

Gross domestic product (2006 est.) U.S. $48.77 billion

Gross domestic product per capita (2006 est.) U.S. $12,000

Life expectancy at birth male 74.43 yr; female 79.74 yr

Major resources hydropower, coffee, bananas, timber, bauxite, cattle, cocoa, gold, iron ore, maize/corn, oranges, rice, silver, sugarcane, sulfur

PANAMA

The Panama Canal links the Pacific and Atlantic Oceans. The trade generated by this engineering feat—a tourist attraction in itself—is the mainstay of the Panamanian economy.

Panama is located between Central and South America. West of the Panama Canal are mountains flanked by coastal plains. East of the canal two mountain arcs run parallel to the Pacific and Caribbean coasts. Most of the country is forested, with rich plant and animal life, and it is generally hot and wet all year.

Panama achieved freedom from Spain in 1821 but remained part of Colombia. The incentive for building the canal was the California Gold Rush of 1849, but the project was only completed in 1914. The United States originally controlled the Canal Zone, but ownership transferred to Panama in 2000. Chief export crops are bananas, coffee, and sugar. Rice and beans are among the staples. Livestock is also important, and Panama is largely self-sufficient in food. Shrimp are a major export. There is industry around Panama City, but most revenue comes from services such as the Panama Canal, the Colón Free Trade Zone, finance, tourism, and Panamanian flag of convenience shipping.

NATIONAL DATA – PANAMA

Land area	75,990 sq km (29,340 sq mi)			
Climate	Altitude m (ft)	Temperatures January °C(°F)	July °C(°F)	Annual precipitation mm (in)
Panama City	36 (118)	26 (79)	27 (81)	2,907 (114.4)

Major physical features highest point: Volcán Barú 3,475 m (11,401 ft); largest lake: Gatún 430 sq km (166 sq mi)

Population (2006 est.) 3,191,319

Form of government multiparty republic with one legislative house

Armed forces paramilitary 11,800

Capital city Panama City (403,808)

Official language Spanish

Ethnic composition Mestizo 70%; Amerindian and mixed (West Indian) 14%; White 10%; Amerindian 6%

Religious affiliations Roman Catholic 85%; Protestant 15%

Currency 1 Panamanian balboa (PAB) = 100 centesimos

Gross domestic product (2006 est.) U.S. $25.29 billion

Gross domestic product per capita (2006 est.) U.S. $7,900

Life expectancy at birth male 72.68 yr; female 77.87 yr

Major resources copper, shrimps, hydropower, tourism, coffee, bananas, cattle, maize/corn, rice, sugarcane, timber

CUBA

The state of Cuba consists of a single long island south of Florida, flanked by the much smaller Isla de la Juventud (Isle of Youth) to the south. The main island has wide stretches of lowland divided by three main mountain areas. The coastline is irregular and is lined with many mangroves, beaches, and coral reefs. The climate is semitropical, with heavy seasonal rainfall and the likelihood of hurricanes. Rivers vary with the seasons, and only a few of them are navigable. Despite much deforestation, the island's forests are still extensive and include tropical near-jungle.

NATIONAL DATA – CUBA

Land area	110,860 sq km (42,803 sq mi)			
Climate		Temperatures		Annual precipitation
	Altitude m (ft)	January °C(°F)	July °C(°F)	mm (in)
Havana	49 (161)	22 (72)	28 (82)	1,189 (46.8)

Major physical features	highest point: Turquino 2,000 m (6,560 ft); longest river: Cauto 249 km (155 mi)
Population	(2006 est.) 11,382,820
Form of government	multiparty republic with one legislative house
Armed forces	army 38,000; navy 3,000; air force 8,000
Largest cities	Havana (capital – 2,164,362); Santiago de Cuba (570,503); Camagüey (355,027); Holguín (330,116); Guantánamo (280,024); Santa Clara (256,184)
Official language	Spanish
Ethnic composition	Mulatto 51%; White 37%; Black 11%; Chinese 1%
Religious affiliations	nonreligious 55.2%; Roman Catholic 39.7%; Afro-Cuban 1.7%; Protestant 3.4%
Currency	1 Cuban peso (CUP) or Convertible peso (CUC) = 100 centavos
Gross domestic product	(2006 est.) U.S. $44.54 billion
Gross domestic product per capita	(2006 est.) U.S. $3,900
Life expectancy at birth	male 75.11 yr; female 79.85 yr
Major resources	cobalt, nickel, iron ore, chromium, copper, salt, timber, silica, petroleum, tourism, beans, cassava, coffee, livestock, maize, oranges, rice, sugarcane, sweet potatoes, tobacco, tropical fruits

Buildings reflecting Cuba's colonial Spanish past in the capital, Havana. The Soviet-style economy imposed on the country by Fidel Castro has held back modernization.

Cuba was an early Spanish settlement, later divided into estates worked by slaves. Independence in 1899 was followed by rule under Fulgencio Batista (1901–73), who was ousted in a coup led by Fidel Castro (b. 1927). Castro's communist regime was backed by Soviet aid until the early 1990s. When this ended, the economy declined and was further damaged by hurricanes in the mid-1990s. The U.S.-imposed economic boycott also depresses the economy. In 2007 Castro's failing health led to rumors of his death.

The main cash crops are sugarcane, tobacco, fruits, and coffee. Nickel is also exported. Traditional industries are food and tobacco processing, and production of steel, machinery, and fertilizers has been introduced. Tourism has become an important revenue earner, surpassed only by money sent back home by Cubans exiled in the United States.

JAMAICA

Apart from the coastal plains and some fertile river basins, Jamaica's land rises sharply to a heavily eroded limestone plateau. Several mountain ranges rise above the plateau, the highest being the Blue Mountains in the east. The climate is mainly tropical. Tropical rain forest still clads the northeastern slopes, but the southern lowlands support only savanna scrub.

Jamaica was settled by the Spanish, who brought slaves to work the land until it was taken by the British in 1655. Jamaica became immensely profitable through its slave-worked sugar plantations, but this prosperity ended with the abolition of slavery in 1833. In 1866 Jamaica became a crown colony, and banana growing was introduced. Full independence was gained in 1962.

Life is harsh for many Jamaicans, and poverty-stricken slums sit side by side with wealthy tourist areas. Rastafarianism, the religio-political movement that regards Ethiopia in Africa as the spiritual homeland of black people, began in Jamaica.

Agriculture has declined but remains important, with sugarcane and bananas being the main cash crops, along with coffee and cocoa. The chief mineral resource is bauxite, and alumina processing is a major industry. Other export activities include printing, textile manufacture, and food processing. Tourism is the major revenue earner. Transportation is generally good.

Jamaica's sandy coastlines are the country's major tourist asset. Tourism provides the largest source of foreign income to the island.

NATIONAL DATA – JAMAICA

Land area	10,831 sq km (4,182 sq mi)			

Climate	Altitude m (ft)	Temperatures January °C(°F)	July °C(°F)	Annual precipitation mm (in)
Kingston	34 (112)	26 (79)	29 (84)	813 (32)

Major physical features	highest point: Blue Mountain Peak 2,256 m (7,402 ft)

Population	(2006 est.) 2,758,124

Form of government multiparty constitutional monarchy with two legislative houses

Armed forces army 2,500; navy 190; air force 140

Capital city Kingston (586,630)

Official language English

Ethnic composition Black 90.9%; East Indian 1.3%; White 0.2%; Chinese 0.2%; Mixed 7.3%; other 0.1%

Religious affiliations Protestant 61.3% (Church of God 21.2%; Seventh-Day Adventist 9%; Baptist 8.8%; Pentecostal 7.6%; Anglican 5.5%; Methodist 2.7%; United Church 2.7%; Jehovah's Witness 1.6%; Brethren 1.1%; Moravian 1.1%); Roman Catholic 4%; other including some spiritual cults 34.7%

Currency 1 Jamaican dollar (JMD) = 100 cents

Gross domestic product (2006 est.) U.S. $12.71 billion

Gross domestic product per capita (2006 est.) U.S. $4,600

Life expectancy at birth male 71.54 yr; female 75.03 yr

Major resources bauxite, gypsum, limestone, rum, coffee, bananas, cocoa, citrus fruits, coconuts, ginger, molasses, pimiento, sugarcane, tourism

BAHAMAS

NATIONAL DATA – BAHAMAS

Land area	10,070 sq km (3,888 sq mi)			
Climate		Temperatures	Annual	
	Altitude m (ft)	January °C(°F)	July °C(°F)	precipitation mm (in)
Nassau	4 (13)	21 (70)	28 (82)	1,389 (54.6)

Major physical features highest point: Cat Island 63 m (206 ft); largest island: Andros 5,957 sq km (2,300 sq mi)

Population (2006 est.) 303,770

Form of government multiparty constitutional monarchy with two legislative houses

Armed forces Royal Bahamian Defense Force 860

Capital city Nassau (235,105)

Official language English

Ethnic composition Black 85%; White 12%; Asian and Hispanic 3%

Religious affiliations Baptist 35.4%; Anglican 15.1%; Roman Catholic 13.5%; Pentecostal 8.1%; Church of God 4.8%; Methodist 4.2%; other Christian 15.2%; none or unspecified 2.9%; other 0.8%

Currency 1 Bahamian dollar (BSD) = 100 cents

Gross domestic product (2006 est.) $6.476 billion

Gross domestic product per capita (2006 est.) $21,300

Life expectancy at birth male 62.24 yr; female 69.03 yr

Major resources salt, calcium carbonate, timber, tourism, fruit and vegetables, limestone, okra, shellfish

Cruise liners at the port of Nassau, the capital of the Bahamas. Tourism is the mainstay of this politically stable chain of islands.

The Bahamas are a long archipelago of about 700 islands and reefs. All are similar, being exposed segments of a single coralline shelf. They are lowlying, apart from a few hills formed from windblown sand, and their coasts are fringed with mangroves, lagoons, and coral reefs. The climate is mild and humid, but rainfall is soon lost through the porous limestone bedrock. Caribbean pine covers much of the larger islands, such as Andros and New Providence. Teeming birds and colorful sealife attract many tourists.

Spanish slave traders removed the indigenous Arawak people and put them to work on Hispaniola. British settlers arrived in the 17th century, and the islands became a British colony in 1629. The Bahamas briefly thrived on illicit trade with the United States during the Civil War (1861–65) and the Prohibition of the 1920s but gained more lasting prosperity from tourism after World War II. Full independence was gained (from Britain) in 1973.

Apart from fruit and vegetable growing, there is little agriculture. Major industries include refining of imported petroleum for export and pharmaceuticals. Services such as tourism and banking (the Bahamas are an important tax haven) account for 90 percent of GDP.

HAITI

One of the world's poorest countries, Haiti consists of two mountainous peninsulas enclosing a central plain. The climate is hot with seasonal rains, but some areas are practically desert. A former slave-worked plantation colony, most of today's population are Creole-speaking descendants of these Africans. Haiti has suffered under brutal dictatorships and revolutions in more recent times, including that of François "Papa Doc" Duvalier (1907–71), who established a police state. Most people depend on subsistence agriculture, but coffee and sugarcane are exported. Developing industries include textiles and electrical goods.

NATIONAL DATA – HAITI

Land area 27,560 sq km (10,641 sq mi)

Climate	Altitude m (ft)	Temperatures January °C(°F)	July °C(°F)	Annual precipitation mm (in)
Port-au-Prince	37 (121)	26 (79)	29 (84)	1,353 (53.2)

Population (2006 est.) 8,308,504

Form of government multiparty republic with two legislative houses

Armed forces no armed forces

Capital city Port-au-Prince (1,321,522)

Official language English

Ethnic composition Black 95%; Mulatto and White 5%

Religious affiliations Roman Catholic 80%; Protestant 16% (Baptist 10%; Pentecostal 4%; Adventist 1%; other 1%); none 1%; other 3% (approximately half the population practices Voodoo)

Currency 1 gourde (HTG) = 100 centimes

Gross domestic product (2006 est.) U.S. $14.56 billion

Gross domestic product per capita (2006 est.) U.S. $1,800

Life expectancy at birth male 51.89 yr; female 54.6 yr

Major resources bauxite, copper, calcium carbonate, gold, marble, hydropower, coffee, sugarcane, bananas, cassava, maize/corn, rice, sisal, sorghum, timber

DOMINICAN REPUBLIC

The Dominican Republic occupies the eastern part of Hispaniola (the western part is occupied by Haiti). The mountainous landscape is interspersed with extensive lowlands. The climate is mainly tropical with seasonal rains, but while some regions have lush forests, others are arid scrubland. A turbulent political past saw democratic elections for the first time in 1978. Ferronickel is now the major export, replacing the traditional reliance on sugar. Tourism is a major foreign currency earner, and other industries are developing.

NATIONAL DATA – DOMINICAN REPUBLIC

Land area 48,380 sq km (18,680 sq mi)

Climate	Altitude m (ft)	Temperatures January °C(°F)	July °C(°F)	Annual precipitation mm (in)
Santo Domingo	17 (56)	24 (76)	27 (81)	1,447 (56.9)

Major physical features highest point: Pico Duarte 3,175 m (10,417 ft)

Population (2006 est.) 9,183,984

Form of government multiparty republic with two legislative houses

Armed forces army 15,000; navy 4,000; air force 5,500

Largest cities Santo Domingo (capital – 2,306,138); Santiago (589,358); San Pedro de Macoris (235,467)

Official language Spanish

Ethnic composition Mixed 73%; White 16%; Black 11%

Religious affiliations Roman Catholic 95%; other 5%

Currency 1 Dominican peso (DOP) = 100 centavos

Gross domestic product (2006 est.) U.S. $73.74 billion

Gross domestic product per capita (2006 est.) U.S. $8,000

Life expectancy at birth male 70.21 yr; female 73.33 yr

Major resources nickel, bauxite, gold, silver, tourism, ferronickel, cocoa, coffee, cotton, flowers, mangoes, maize/corn, oranges, platinum, rice, salt, sugar beet, tobacco, tomatoes

SAINT KITTS AND NEVIS

Saint Kitts and Nevis form part of the western chain of the Leeward Islands. The volcanic mountainous interiors have lush vegetation, but the lower slopes have been cleared for cultivation. The main cash crops are sugarcane on Saint Kitts and cotton and coconuts on Nevis. Other major industries include footwear, fabrics, electronics, offshore banking, and data processing equipment. Tourism is the main revenue earner, however, with visitors attracted to the fine beaches. There are good roads and ferry connections, a deepwater harbor, and an airport on each island.

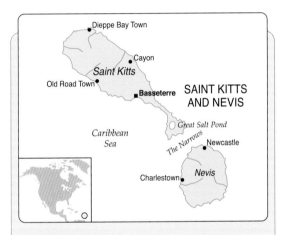

NATIONAL DATA – SAINT KITTS AND NEVIS

Land area 261 sq km (101 sq mi)

Climate	Altitude m (ft)	Temperatures January °C(°F)	July °C(°F)	Annual precipitation mm (in)
Basseterre	15 (49)	24 (75)	27 (81)	1,375 (54.2)

Major physical features highest point: Mount Misery 1,156 m (3,792 ft)

Population (2006 est.) 39,129

Form of government multiparty constitutional monarchy with one legislative house

Armed forces no armed forces

Capital city Basseterre (12,849)

Official language English

Ethnic composition Black 90.5%; Mixed 5.0%; Indian 3.0%; White 1.5%

Religious affiliations Protestant 76.4%; Roman Catholic 10.7%; other 12.9%

Currency 1 East Caribbean dollar (ECD) = 100 cents

Gross domestic product (2002 est.) U.S. $339 million

Gross domestic product per capita (2005 est.) U.S. $8,200

Life expectancy at birth male 69.56 yr; female 75.42 yr

Major resources tourism, coconuts, livestock, sugarcane, vegetables, cotton

ANTIGUA AND BARBUDA

These two small islands, part of the Leeward Islands, are of strategic importance to the United States, which operates military bases here. Antigua has been mostly deforested, but the coral island of Barbuda is well wooded. The climate is warm and humid, but water is scarce. The islands are subject to hurricanes. Tourism is the main revenue earner; there are numerous white, palm-fringed beaches and a number of casinos, as well as fine architecture in the capital, St. John's. Offshore financial services have also become important.

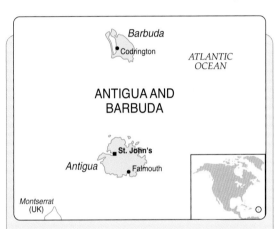

NATIONAL DATA – ANTIGUA AND BARBUDA

Land area 443 sq km (171 sq mi)

Climate	Altitude m (ft)	Temperatures January °C(°F)	July °C(°F)	Annual precipitation mm (in)
St. John's	10 (33)	25 (77)	28 (83)	1,052 (41.4)

Major physical features highest point: Boggy Peak 405 m (1,330 ft); largest island: Antigua 280 sq km (108 sq mi)

Population (2006 est.) 69,108

Form of government multiparty constitutional monarchy with two legislative houses

Armed forces army 125; navy 45

Capital city St. John's (25,498)

Official language English

Ethnic composition Black 94.4%; Mulatto 3.5%; White 1.3%; others 0.8%

Religious affiliations Anglican 33%; other Protestants 31%; Roman Catholic 12%; other 23%; none 1%

Currency 1 East Caribbean dollar (ECD) = 100 cents

Gross domestic product (2002 est.) U.S. $750 million

Gross domestic product per capita (2005 est.) U.S. $10,900

Life expectancy at birth male 69.78 yr; female 74.66 yr

Major resources tourism, cotton, rum, shellfish, sugarcane, vegetables, fruit, chickens

DOMINICA

Situated in the Leeward Islands chain, Dominica has a backbone of steep volcanic mountains. The climate is warm and humid, with the risk of hurricanes. Lush tropical vegetation supports abundant wildlife, and the Morne Trois Pitons National Park is an important tourist attraction. Dominica is relatively poor compared with its neighbors, and the end of preferential treatment for Dominican bananas entering the EU caused concern. Other agricultural exports include citrus fruits and vanilla. Galvanized sheets and coconut products are also exported. Nearly one-quarter of the workforce is unemployed, and subsidies from the World Trade Organization help support the economy.

NATIONAL DATA - DOMINICA

Land area	754 sq km (291 sq mi)			
Climate		Temperatures		Annual
	Altitude m (ft)	January °C(°F)	July °C(°F)	precipitation mm (in)
Roseau	16 (60)	24 (75)	27 (81)	1,981 (77.9)

Major physical features	highest point: Morne Diablotin 1,447 m (4,747 ft)

Population (2006 est.) 68,910

Form of government multiparty republic with one legislative house

Armed forces no armed forces

Capital city Roseau (16,582)

Official language English

Ethnic composition Black 91.2%; Mixed 6.6%; Amerindian 1.5%; White 0.5%; others 0.2%

Religious affiliations Roman Catholic 80%; Protestant 16%; other 4%

Currency 1 East Caribbean dollar (ECD) = 100 cents

Gross domestic product (2003 est.) U.S. $384 million

Gross domestic product per capita (2005 est.) U.S. $3,800

Life expectancy at birth male 71.95 yr; female 77.93 yr

Major resources timber, hydropower, bananas, cattle, cocoa, coconuts, citrus fruits, pigs, pumice, tourism, vanilla

SAINT LUCIA

Saint Lucia is part of the Lesser Antilles chain that stretches from Puerto Rico to Venezuela. The island's rugged landscape is the result of volcanic activity. The climate is hot and humid, and the volcanic soils are fertile. The once lush rain forest has been cleared from the island. Saint Lucia gained independence from Britain in 1979. The economy depends mainly on tourism—the country's largest single employer—and agriculture. Bananas are no longer the main crop; the end of EU preference for bananas from the Caribbean islands seriously damaged the Saint Lucia economy. Industry is developing, aided by geothermal power.

NATIONAL DATA - SAINT LUCIA

Land area	606 sq km (234 sq mi)			
Climate		Temperatures		Annual
	Altitude m (ft)	January °C(°F)	July °C(°F)	precipitation mm (in)
Castries	3 (10	25 (77)	27 (81)	2,199 (86.5)

Major physical features	highest point: Mount Gimie 950 m (3,117 ft)

Population (2006 est.) 168,458

Form of government multiparty constitutional monarchy with two legislative houses

Armed forces no armed forces

Capital city Castries (12,819)

Official language English

Ethnic composition Black 90%; Mixed 6%; East Indian 3%; White 1%

Religious affiliations Roman Catholic 75%; Protestant 13%; Hindu 1%; other 11%

Currency 1 East Caribbean dollar (ECD) = 100 cents

Gross domestic product (2002 est.) U.S. $866 million

Gross domestic product per capita (2005 est.) U.S. $4,800

Life expectancy at birth male 70.29 yr; female 77.65 yr

Major resources timber, minerals (pumice), geothermal potential, bananas, cocoa, coconuts, fruit, spices, vegetables, tourism

BARBADOS

Barbados is founded on coral deposits around a rocky core. Although hilly in the north and center, there are extensive sandy beaches and plenty of trees on the island. Modern settlement was begun by British sugar planters in the 17th century, and present-day Barbadians are descended from their slaves. The island became independent in 1966. Agriculture is dominated by sugarcane and its by-products, such as molasses and rum. Other crops include cotton and fruits. Small gas and petroleum reserves are exploited, and light industries produce electrical components and clothing. Data processing, banking, and insurance are growing. Tourism is the biggest single currency earner, however.

NATIONAL DATA - BARBADOS

Land area	431 sq km (166 sq mi)			
Climate		Temperatures		Annual precipitation
	Altitude m (ft)	January °C(°F)	July °C(°F)	mm (in)
Bridgetown	55 (180)	25 (77)	27 (81)	1,278 (50)

Major physical features highest point: Mount Hillaby 337 m (1,104 ft)

Population (2006 est.) 279,912

Form of government multiparty constitutional monarchy with two legislative houses

Armed forces army 500; navy 110

Capital city Bridgetown (98,947)

Official language English

Ethnic composition Black 90%; White 4%; Asian and mixed 6%

Religious affiliations Protestant 31%; other Anglican 29%; other Christian 24%; Roman Catholic 4%; other 12%

Currency 1 Barbadian dollar (BDS) = 100 cents

Gross domestic product (2006 est.) $5.108 billion

Gross domestic product per capita (2006 est.) $18,200

Life expectancy at birth male 70.79 yr; female 74.82 yr

Major resources bananas, fish, goats, limestone, natural gas, petroleum, onions, pigs, poultry, shellfish, sheep, sugarcane, vegetables, tourism, cotton

ST. VINCENT AND THE GRENADINES

These islands form part of the Windward Islands in the Lesser Antilles. Saint Vincent is a thickly forested cluster of volcanic mountains, the highest peak of which is still active. The Grenadines are lowlying coral islands. Independence was gained in 1979. Arrowroot is now the chief crop—used for making medicines, flour, and paper. Upmarket tourism is being encouraged in the Grenadines, and offshore finance is increasing. The country also gains revenue from flag of convenience shipping. There are also various light industries.

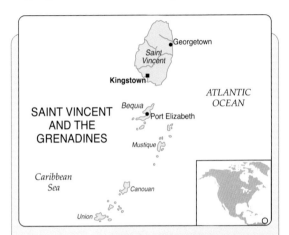

NATIONAL DATA –SAINT VINCENT AND THE GRENADINES

Land area	389 sq km (150 sq mi)			
Climate		Temperatures		Annual precipitation
	Altitude m (ft)	January °C(°F)	July °C(°F)	mm (in)
Kingstown	1 (3)	26 (45)	28 (77)	1,524 (60)

Major physical features highest point: Soufrière 1,234 m (4,048 ft); largest island: Saint Vincent 344 sq km (133 sq mi)

Population (2006 est.) 117,848

Form of government multiparty constitutional monarchy with one legislative house

Armed forces no armed forces

Capital city Kingstown (18,323)

Official language English

Ethnic composition Black 66%; Mixed 19%; East Indian 6%; Carib Amerindian 2%; other 7%

Religious affiliations Anglican 47%; Methodist 28%; Roman Catholic 13%; Hindu, Seventh-Day Adventist; other Protestant 12%

Currency 1 East Caribbean dollar (ECD) = 100 cents

Gross domestic product (2002 est.) U.S. $342 million

Gross domestic product per capita (2005 est.) U.S. $3,600

Life expectancy at birth male 71.99 yr; female 75.77 yr

Major resources hydropower, arrowroot, starch, bananas, coconuts, spices, taro, timber, tourism

GRENADA

Grenada lies in the Lesser Antilles. The territory also includes the southernmost islands of the Grenadines. Grenada, which suffered serious hurricane damage in 2004, consists mainly of thickly forested volcanic peaks, but the southern coasts have many bays and harbors, including the capital, St. George's. The people are mainly descended from former African slaves. Grenada became independent in 1974. Tourism is now the single most important industry; cruise ships regularly visit the island, and there is a growing hotel sector. Offshore financial services are also among the service sector industries that now make up nearly 70 percent of GDP.

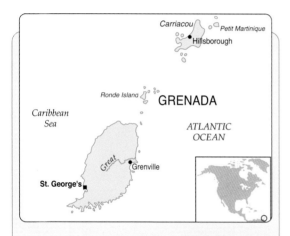

NATIONAL DATA – GRENADA

Land area   344 sq km (133 sq mi)

Climate	Altitude m (ft)	Temperatures January °C(°F)	July °C(°F)	Annual precipitation mm (in)
St. George's	1 (3)	25 (77)	27 (81)	1,560 (61.4))

Major physical features   highest point: Mount St. Catherine 840 m (2,757 ft)

Population   (2006 est.) 89,703

Form of government   multiparty constitutional monarchy with two legislative houses

Armed forces   no armed forces

Capital city   St. George's (4,298)

Official language   English

Ethnic composition   Black 82%; Mixed Black and European 13%; European and East Indian 5%

Religious affiliations   Roman Catholic 53%; Anglican 13.8%; other Protestant 33.2%

Currency   1 East Caribbean dollar (ECD) = 100 cents

Gross domestic product   (2002 est.) U.S. $440 million

Gross domestic product per capita   (2005 est.) U.S. $3,900

Life expectancy at birth   male 63.06 yr; female 66.68 yr

Major resources   timber, tropical fruits, cocoa, vegetables, mace, nutmeg, tourism

TRINIDAD AND TOBAGO

Venezuela's coastal mountains continue into both Trinidad (which also has rolling plains, swamps, and rain forests) and Tobago (which has coral plains extending out to sea). The climate is hot and humid. Formerly a slave-worked colony, independence was gained in 1962. Calypso music and carnival bring a vibrant culture to the islands. The economy depends on refining and exporting petroleum reserves, but falls in oil prices have led to diversification into other sectors. Tourism is a key industry. Agricultural cash crops include sugarcane, coffee, and cocoa.

NATIONAL DATA – TRINIDAD AND TOBAGO

Land area   5,128 sq km (1,980 sq mi)

Climate	Altitude m (ft)	Temperatures January °C(°F)	July °C(°F)	Annual precipitation mm (in)
Port-of-Spain	20 (66)	26 (77)	27 (81)	1,408 (55.4)

Major physical features   highest point: Mount Aripo 940 m (3,084 ft)

Population   (2006 est.) 1,065,842

Form of government   multiparty republic with two legislative houses

Armed forces   army 2,000 navy 700

Capital city   Port-of-Spain (49,865)

Official language   English

Ethnic composition   Indian (South Asian) 40%; African 37.5%; Mixed 20.5%; other 1.2%; unspecified 0.8%

Religious affiliations   Roman Catholic 26%; Hindu 22.5%; Anglican 7.8%; Baptist 7.2%; Pentecostal 6.8%; other Christian 5.8%; Muslim 5.8%; Seventh-Day Adventist 4%; other 10.8%; unspecified 1.4%; none 1.9%

Currency   1 Trinidad and Tobago dollar (TTD) = 100 cents

Gross domestic product   (2006 est.) U.S. $20.99 billion

Gross domestic product per capita   (2006 est.) U.S. $19,700

Life expectancy at birth   male 65.71 yr; female 67.86 yr

Major resources   asphalt, bananas, citrus fruits, cocoa, coffee, oil and natural gas, rice, sugarcane, tourism

Anguilla

Overseas Territory of the United Kingdom

The northernmost of the Leeward Islands in the Caribbean, Anguilla is a long thin coral island with scrubland and occasional fruit plantations. The climate is warm and humid and subject to hurricanes. Anguilla has been a British colony since 1650. The governor is appointed by the crown, but internal affairs are managed by an elected assembly. Most Anguillans are descended from former African slaves. English is the chief language, and the main religion is Christianity. The key exports are fish, salt, and livestock. There are significant saltpeter deposits but few other resources. Tourism is being developed. Expatriate Anguillans in the U.S. Virgin Islands and the UK outnumber residents, and remittances are a major source of income.

Aruba

Part of the Kingdom of the Netherlands

The island of Aruba lies at the southwestern end of the Lesser Antilles. The land is mostly flat with volcanic boulders. The climate is warm and humid, but rainfall is low, and vegetation consists of cacti and succulents. Aruba became part of the Netherlands Antilles in 1634, but seceded in 1986, becoming an internally self-governing part of the Netherlands. The monarch is represented by a governor, but the 21 members of the States of Aruba are directly elected. Arubans are mainly of African, European, and Asian descent, and most are Roman Catholic. Dutch is the official language. Tourism is the major source of revenue, but offshore banking, financial services, and data processing also account for a large service-sector economy.

Bermuda

Overseas Territory of the United Kingdom

Bermuda occupies a string of coral islands in the North Atlantic. About 20 are inhabited, the largest being Bermuda. The climate is warm, mild, and humid, with moderate rainfall. Vegetation is luxuriant. Bermuda became a colony of the British Virginia Company in 1612. It passed to the crown in 1684 but remained self-governing. The House of Assembly is directly elected, but the Senate is chosen by the governor, appointed by

A male green iguana on Aruba. The warm, dry climate is well suited to reptiles such as these.

the British crown. Most people are descended from former African slaves. The official language is English, and Christianity is the dominant religion. There is little agriculture or large-scale industry, and food and fuel are imported. Tourism is the largest employer, catering to the luxury market and drawing about 80 percent of visitors from the United States. Since the 1990s there has been a massive growth in offshore financial services, banking, and insurance, and Bermuda is now one of the principal reinsurance centers. Living standards are among the highest in the world, and there are well developed education and welfare services.

British Virgin Islands

Overseas Territory of the United Kingdom

A British colony comprising Tortola, Anegada, Virgin Gorda, Jost Van Dyke, and more than 30 islets of the Virgin Islands group in the Caribbean. Most are the peaks of submerged mountains, and they have a subtropical climate. The original Arawak inhabitants were driven out by Caribs, who in turn were wiped out by the Spanish. The islands became a pirate haven until annexed by Britain in the 17th century. Tourism is expanding to dominate the economy; the sheltered waters attract a great number of visitors. Agriculture produces livestock for local use, and cash and food crops such as bananas and sugarcane. Fishing is important, but manufacturing industry is very small scale. Despite water shortages, healthcare is excellent.

Cayman Islands
Overseas Territory of the United Kingdom
These islands are a British colony in the Caribbean, northwest of Jamaica. Cayman Brac and Little Cayman are lowlying coral islands on a rocky base. The coasts have magnificent beaches and reefs and a tropical climate cooled by sea breezes. More or less a pirate haven until ceded to Britain with Jamaica in 1670, the Caymans became a separate colony after Jamaican independence in 1962. There is little agriculture or industry. Tourism is a major earner, and banking secrecy laws and lack of direct taxation have encouraged the fast growth of financial services. More than 40,000 companies are registered in the Caymans. The service sector employs 95 percent of the labor force.

Greenland
Self-governing Overseas Administrative Division of Denmark
At 2,175,600 sq km (840,325 sq mi) in area, Greenland is the world's largest island. About 85 percent of this cold landmass lying within the Arctic Circle is covered by the northern hemisphere's biggest ice cap. At its edges, glaciers have formed a landscape of fjords and islands. The climate is arctic. Wildlife and vegetation in the ice-free areas are typical of the Arctic tundra. There are salmon and trout in rivers and streams, while cod, salmon, and various flatfish are found offshore. Inuit have lived on Greenland since they reached the area between 4000 B.C. and 1000 A.D. Vikings also established colonies, and Greenland became a Danish colony in 1721. Home rule was

instituted in 1979, but Denmark retains control of foreign affairs, and Greenlanders are Danish citizens. Settlement is limited mainly to the coastal fringe. Sheep and reindeer are reared in the extreme south, where hay is grown for fodder. Fishing has replaced seal-hunting as the leading industry. Hunting in the north produces pelts for export. The large mineral resources are hard to extract, but lead and zinc are mined. A small road network exists, but dog sleds remain the best form of surface transportation.

Guadeloupe
Overseas Department of France
Guadeloupe consists of two groups of islands within the Lesser Antilles in the eastern Caribbean. The main islands are Basse-Terre and Grand-Terre. Basse-Terre is mountainous with an active volcano, while Grand-Terre is mainly lowlying. Vegetation ranges from mangrove swamps on Grand-Terre to dense forests on Basse-Terre. Cacti and dry forest are found on the smaller islands. In 1674 this former Spanish colony passed to the French crown. After falling into British hands it returned to France, and in 1946 Gaudeloupe became an administrative district of France. Most inhabitants are black or mixed-race descendants of slaves. Income from agriculture, tourism, and industry leaves a large deficit, made up by grants from France.

Martinique
Overseas Department of France
Martinique is a Caribbean island in the Lesser Antilles, between Dominica and Saint Lucia. Mountainous and volcanic, the island is dominated by Mount Pelée in the north. The basin of the Lézarde River is the only significant lowland area. The hot, humid climate encourages lush vegetation, with tropical rain forests and coastal mangrove swamps. Caribs killed the indigenous Arawak peoples. In the 17th century the island was settled by French sugarcane growers. They imported large numbers of African slaves, who were not freed until 1848. After World War II Martinique became beset with economic problems. These have given birth to a vociferous independence movement, which has led to several terrorist campaigns on mainland France. But

because of its chronic trade imbalance, the island relies on France, and so true independence seems unlikely. Agriculture and tourism are the mainstays. The banana trade has benefited from France's EU membership. Other crops include sugarcane and exotic flowers. Industry is mainly in the form of food processing.

Montserrat

Overseas Territory of the United Kingdom

Montserrat is one of the Leeward Islands in the eastern Caribbean. Volcanic peaks, several still active, dominate a mountainous landscape. Montserrat was colonized by Irish settlers from nearby Saint Kitts in the 17th century. Most people are descendants of former African slaves. Volcanic eruptions since 1995 have covered two-thirds of the island in volcanic dust, ash, and lava, damaging the economy, which was based on tourism and cotton and vegetable exports. Half the island was completely evacuated, with islanders migrating to other islands and to Britain. Some islanders later went back, but the return of others is prevented by lack of housing. About half the island remains an exclusion zone.

Netherland Antilles

Part of the Kingdom of the Netherlands

The Netherlands Antilles are made up of two island groups in the Lesser Antilles. The southern islands are generally flat, but those in the north are mountainous and volcanic. The vegetation is sparse apart from cacti and succulents. The people are mainly of African and European descent. Petroleum and its derivatives are the main exports, and the famous Curaçao liqueur is also exported. Tourism and banking are also important sources of revenue. It is expected that soon some of the islands will have a different constitutional status and others will be reincorporated into the Netherlands as Dutch municipalities.

Puerto Rico

Unincorporated Organized Territory of the United States

Most of the main island is upland, rising from the southern coastal plains of the Cordillera Central, a mountain range that runs along the island like a

backbone; in the north it flattens to hill country. The two adjoining islands are also rugged. The north gets most of the rainfall and is dotted with marshes, lakes, and mangrove swamps, but the tropical rain forest that once covered most of the island has nearly all been cleared. Puerto Rico was once a Spanish possession, and slaves were brought in to work the plantations until the abolition of slavery in the 19th century. The people were given U.S. citizenship in 1919, but the islands' culture has remained mainly Hispanic.

Puerto Rico is one of the Caribbean's most prosperous countries. Densely populated, there has been large-scale migration to the United States. The main cash crops are sugarcane, tobacco, and coffee; dairy products and livestock are also important. Industry includes plastics, petrochemicals, textiles, machinery, and electronics. Although exports are high, especially to the United States, imports are also high.

San Juan Bay, Puerto Rico. This island state in the West Indies is a self-governing commonwealth in association with the United States.

Tourism has become a major revenue earner. Social security and welfare benefits operate to U.S. standards, and healthcare is rapidly improving.

Saint-Pierre and Miquelon
Territorial Collectivity of France
This tiny archipelago off the coast of Newfoundland was first settled by French fishermen in the 17th century. The largest island, Miquelon, consists of two islands linked by an isthmus. Saint-Pierre is smaller but accommodates most of the population. The scenery is barren, with few trees and extensive peat bogs. The tall cliffs and rocky islets attract many seabirds. The islands achieved their present status in 1985. The population has remained staunchly French, voting in both local and French national elections. A few vegetables are grown for local consumption, but the economy relies on fishing in the rich waters nearby. There is free education and good health and welfare provision.

Turks and Caicos Islands
Overseas Territory of the United Kingdom
The Turks and Caicos Islands are about 30 small islands at the end of the Bahamas group, which they resemble in landscape and climate. The terrain is dry, and the vegetation is scrubby except in the coastal saltmarshes. The inhabitants are descended from African slaves imported by the British in the 17th century to work the saltpans. The islands have on several occasions been annexed to the Bahamas and to Jamaica. In 1976 they were granted self-government under the British crown. Salt production has become uneconomic, and agriculture is hindered by lack of water. Thus the islands' economy rests mainly on fishing and on the development of tourism. Many offshore financial companies are based here, taking advantage of the islands' status as a tax haven.

Virgin Islands
Unincorporated Organized Territory of the United States
The islands comprise St. Croix, St. John, and St. Thomas and about 50 smaller islands of the Virgin Islands group east of Puerto Rico. Their rugged landscapes are formed by the peaks of an undersea mountain range. The islands were settled by the Spanish and French before being acquired by Denmark in the 17th and 18th centuries. African slaves were introduced to work the sugarcane plantations. In 1917 the islands were bought by the United States. A constitution in 1981 introduced self-government to the islands with an elected governor and senate. Agriculture has shifted from sugarcane to food crops and livestock, mostly for domestic use. Manufacturing ranges from rum distilling to petroleum refining, and the islands' free port status has also encouraged industrial development. Tourism dominates the economy—game fishing is one of the major attractions. Education and healthcare are widely available, reflecting the islands' relative prosperity.

GLOSSARY

Words in SMALL CAPITALS refer to other entries in the Glossary.

Amerindian A member of one of the many INDIGENOUS PEOPLES of Central and South America.

Anglican A member of the PROTESTANT church—founded in England in the 16th century—including the Church of England and other churches throughout the world.

apartheid A way of organizing society to keep racial groups apart. Introduced after 1948 in South Africa by the National Party to ensure continued white political dominance, it has now been dismantled.

Buddhism A religion founded in India in the 6th and 5th centuries B.C. and based on the teachings of Gautama Siddhartha (c. 563-483 B.C.), the Buddha, or "Awakened One."

cereal A cultivated grass selectively bred to produce high yields of edible grain for consumption by humans and livestock. The most important are wheat (*Triticum*), rice (*Oryza sativa*), and maize/corn (*Zea mays*).

Christianity A religion based on the teachings of Jesus Christ and originating from JUDAISM in the 1st century A.D. Its main beliefs are found in the Bible, and it is now the world's most widespread religion, divided into a number of churches and sects, including ROMAN CATHOLICISM, PROTESTANTISM, and ORTHODOX CHURCHES.

Communism A social and economic system based on the communal ownership of property. It usually refers to the STATE-controlled social and economic systems in the former Soviet Union and Soviet bloc countries and in the People's Republic of China.

Confucianism A religion or moral code based on the teachings of the Chinese philosopher Confucius (c. 551-479 B.C.) that formed the foundations of Chinese imperial administration and ethical behavior; also followed in Korea and other east Asian countries.

constitution The fundamental statement of laws that defines the way a country is governed.

constitutional monarchy A form of government with a hereditary head of STATE or monarch and a CONSTITUTION.

democracy A form of government in which policy is made by the people (direct democracy) or on their behalf (indirect democracy). Indirect democracy usually takes the form of competition among political parties at elections.

Dependency (1) A territorial unit under the jurisdiction of another STATE but not formally annexed to it. **(2)** An unequal economic or political relationship between two states or groups of states, in which one side is dependent on and supports the other.

ethnic group A group of people sharing a social or cultural identity based on language, religion, customs and/or common descent or kinship.

EU (European Union) An alliance of European NATIONS formed to agree common policies in the areas of trade, aid, agriculture, and economics.

exports Goods or services sold to other countries.

federalism A form of CONSTITUTIONAL government in which power is shared between two levels—a central, or federal, government and a tier of provincial or STATE governments.

GDP (Gross Domestic Product) The total value of a country's annual output of goods and services with allowances made for depreciation.

Hinduism A religion originating in India in the 2nd millennium B.C. It emphasizes mystical contemplation and ascetic practices that are closely interwoven with much of Indian culture.

indigenous peoples The original inhabitants of a region.

Islam A religion based on the revelations of God to the prophet Muhammad in the 7th century A.D., as recorded in the Qu'ran. It teaches submission to the will of God and is practiced throughout the Middle East, North Africa, and parts of Southeast Asia.

Judaism A religion that developed in ancient Israel based on God's law and revelations declared to Moses on Mount Sinai.

Methodism A PROTESTANT denomination of the CHRISTIAN church based on the teachings of the English theologian John Wesley (1703-91).

monarch A form of rule where there is a hereditary head of STATE.

Muslim An adherent of ISLAM.

nation A community that believes it consists of a single people, based on historical and cultural criteria.

nation-state A STATE in which the inhabitants all belong to one NATION. Most states claim to be nation-states; in practice almost all of them include minority groups.

Native American The INDIGENOUS PEOPLES of North America.

official language The language used by governments, schools, courts, and other official institutions in countries where the population has no single common mother tongue.

one-party state A political system in which there is no competition to the government party at elections, as in COMMUNIST and military regimes.

parliamentary democracy A political system in which the legislature (Parliament) is elected by all the adult members of the population and the government is formed by the party that commands a majority in the Parliament.

Protestant Term describing CHRISTIAN denominations that share a common rejection of the authority of the pope as head of the church, and of many ROMAN CATHOLIC practices.

Roman Catholic The largest of the CHRISTIAN churches, headed by the pope in Rome. It traces its origin and authority to St. Peter, one of the disciples of Jesus Christ and the first bishop of Rome. There are believers on all continents.

Shi'ite Muslim A member of the smaller of the two main divisions of ISLAM. Followers recognize Muhammad's son-in-law, Ali, and his descendants, the imams (prayer leaders), as his true successors and legitimate leaders of Islam.

state The primary political unit of the modern world, usually defined by its possession of sovereignty over a territory and its people.

subtropical The climatic zone between the TROPICS and TEMPERATE zones. There are marked seasonal changes of temperature but it is never very cold.

Sunni Muslim A member of the larger of the two main divisions of ISLAM. Its members recognize the Caliphs as the successors to Muhammad and follow the *sunna*, or way of the prophet, as recorded in the *hadithw*, the teachings of Muhammad.

temperate climate Any one of the climatic zones in mid-latitudes, with a mild climate. They cover areas between the warm TROPICS and cold polar regions.

tropics (tropical) The area between the Tropic of Cancer (23°30'N) and the Tropic of Capricorn (23°30'S), marking the lines of latitude farthest from the equator where the Sun is still found directly overhead at midday in midsummer.

FURTHER REFERENCES

General Reference Books

Allen, J. L., *Student Atlas of World Geography*, McGraw-Hill, Columbus, OH, 2004.

Atlas of World Geography, Rand McNally, Chicago, IL, 2005.

Baines, J. D., Egan, V., and G. Bateman, *The Encyclopedia of World Geography: A Country by Country Guide*, Thunder Bay, San Diego, CA, 2003.

de Blij, H. J., and P. O. Muller, *Concepts and Regions in Geography*, John Wiley & Sons, New York, 2004.

Muller, P. O., and E. Muller-Hames, *Geography, Study Guide: Realms, Regions, and Concepts*, John Wiley & Sons, New York, 2005.

Oxford Atlas of the World, Oxford University Press, New York, 2003.

Parsons, J. (ed.), *Geography of the World*, DK Children, London and New York, 2006.

Peoples of the World: Their Cultures, Traditions, and Ways of Life, National Geographic, Washington, DC, 2001.

Pulsipher, L. M., *World Regional Geography: Global Patterns, Local Lives*, W. H. Freeman, New York, 2005.

Warf, B. (ed.), *Encyclopedia of Human Geography*, Sage Publications, London and New York, 2006.

Specific to this volume

Bakvis, H., and G. Skogstad (eds.), *Canadian Federalism: Performance, Effectiveness and Legitimacy*, Oxford University Press, Oxford, UK, 2001.

Birdsall, S. S., Palka, E. J., and J. C. Malinowski, *Regional Landscapes of the United States and Canada*, John Wiley & Sons, New York, 2004.

de Blij, H. J., *Atlas of the United States*, Oxford University Press, New York, 2006.

Blouet, B. W., and O. M. Blouet, *Latin America and the Caribbean: A Systematic and Regional Survey*, John Wiley & Sons, New York, 2005.

Bone, R. M., *The Geography of the Canadian North*, Oxford University Press, New York, 2003.

Cummings, Jr., M. C., and D. Wise, *Democracy under Pressure: An Introduction to the American Political System* (9th edn.), International Thomson Publishing, Cambridge, MA, 2001.

Goode's Atlas of North America, John Wiley & Sons, New York, 2004.

Kent, R. B., *Latin America: Regions and People*, The Guilford Press, New York, 2006.

Kotkin, J., and S. Moyers (eds.), *The New Geography: How the Digital Revolution Is Reshaping the American Landscape*, Random House, New York, 2001.

Lopez, B., *Arctic Dreams: Imagination and Desire in a Northern Landscape*, Vintage Books, London, 2001.

McKnight, T. L., *Regional Geography of the United States and Canada* (4th edn.), Prentice Hall, Upper Saddle River, NJ, 2003.

Nash, G. B., et al. (eds.), *The American People* (volumes I and II), Longman, New York, 2005.

Place, S. E. (ed.), *Tropical Rainforest: Latin American Nature and Society in Transition* (Jaguar Books on Latin America, No. 2), Scholarly Resources, Wilmington, DE, 2001.

Wiarda, H. J., *The Soul of Latin America: The Cultural and Political Tradition*, Yale University Press, New Haven, CT, 2003.

Yeates, M., *The North American City* (5th edn.), Harper & Row, New York, 1997.

Web Sites

www.ethnologue.com
A comprehensive guide to all the languages of the world.

www.factmonster.com/ipka/A0770414.html
Geography facts and figures for kids.

www.geographic.org
Information on geography for students, teachers, parents, and children.

www.odci.gov/cia/publications/factbook/index.html
Central Intelligence Agency factbook of country profiles.

ww.panda.org
World Wide Fund for Nature (WWF).

www.peoplegroups.org/default.aspx
Listing and information on major ethnic groups around the world.

www.worldatlas.com
A world atlas of facts, flags, and maps.